essentials

essentials is a series of books specially designed for readers who want to gain an overview of a topic in a short time. These books contain the essence of what is considered "state of the art" in the current professional discussion and in practice. essentials in-form are quick, straightforward and easy to understand. They help

- as an introduction to a current topic,
- as an introduction to a still unknown subject area,
- as insight to have a say on a particular topic.

Uwe G. Seebacher, Julián Garritz

Data-driven Management

A primer for modern corporate decision making

First edition 2021

© AQPS Inc. 2021

Uwe Seebacher
Graz, Austria

Julián Garritz
Frankfurt, Germany

What you can find in this *essential*

- An introduction to the current situation and the importance of data-driven management (DDM)
- Various short definitions of relevant terms in the context of DDM
- A tool for status analysis on DDM in an organization
- A process model for the development or optimization of an already existing system to DDM
- The Quick Check for the self-assessment to determine the own DDM-Readiness but also the respective organizational DDM-potentials
- Brief presentation of various templates and tools that have been tested and are relevant in connection with the development or optimization of DDM
- An outlook on the further development of DDM
- Many further links to articles and sources to deepen the content in this *essential*

Foreword

For many years I have been dealing with the topic of data-driven management (DDM). Conversely, it is also the case that this topic has already occupied me through many years, as it fascinates me. However, until now it has always been the limits of technological feasibility that made modern data-driven management in the context of predictive intelligence seem impossible. In recent years, however, the environment has developed significantly into a positive one with regard to the topic of data-driven management.

Buzzwords like *Big Data, Artificial Intelligence, Blockchain, Marketing Automation* and many others open up almost unlimited possibilities. The current situation reminds me a little of the spirit of optimism when the first systems in the field of customer relationship management (CRM) came onto the market. I still remember how I was involved as an expert in such projects for many different customers. To my regret, however, I must also remember that the majority of these projects were ultimately only half-heartedly thought through and completed. This is confirmed by recent surveys conducted by renowned institutes, which show that around 80% of these systems still fail to deliver the expected added value for their users.

Against this background, I am frightened by statements from more and more managers who are actively evaluating the procurement of a solution in the field of artificial intelligence, in the belief that this will solve the current situation with regard to the data technology blind flight of their own organizations in one fell swoop. This omni-present blind flight was once again made evident by the study published in 2020 by Fujitsu and Freeform Dynamics under the title "The road to becoming a data-driven business", according to which just 5% (!) of companies can be considered "data-driven" today.

Again, I use the comparison of children in elementary school in the context of lectures and talks and refer in this context to how these children are still taught arithmetic today. In the first step they have to learn the basic mechanisms of mathematics by mental arithmetic. Only when they have reached the appropriate level of mathematical maturity do they begin to learn and process more complex arithmetic operations with the calculator. This principle has been used in modern education for many decades, probably not without reason. Therefore, the question arises why such basic principles of logic and learning should not be relevant for much more complex topics.

The conclusion from this is that the handling of artificial intelligence as a pars pro toto of a highly developed technology landscape must first be understood and processed in terms of the underlying mechanisms, logics and algorithms. In addition, it is necessary in the sense of sustainable data-based management to be aware of the three core factors of objectivity, reliability and validity in relation to the data used as content constructs. Quite simply, it is a matter of understanding and being able to recognize whether the available data is valid and reliable. However, this requires an intensive process in terms of working with these data.

Because what can happen in the worst case is that non-valid data is fed into an artificial intelligence system, which then generates supposedly reliable and valid information for far-reaching operational or even strategic corporate decisions. I do not think it is necessary to elaborate further on the fatality of such a situation in terms of responsibility but also entrepreneurial risk.

Against the background of many different projects and research work, I have therefore designed and published a model for the evaluation but also for the development of a data-driven management. In many different projects and initiatives this procedure model was tested and refined. With this process model for data-driven management, you can create the basis for sustainable entrepreneurial success in the context of data-driven management and predictive intelligence step by step without external experts and separate investments for and in your own organization.

With the help of the simple self-testing procedure for DDM, you can evaluate the initial situation before starting the activities and based on this, initiate the first measures while making the best possible use of the things already available in your own organization. I wish you much success on this fascinating journey towards data-driven management. I am convinced that after only a short time you will be just as fascinated by the possibilities that are sure to open up as I have been for years.

April 2021   Uwe Seebacher, Julián Garritz

Table of contents

1 The procedure model for DDM 15
    1.1   The maturity model on DDM 15
    1.2   Phase 1: Reactive-static business analytics 16
        1.2.1   It's all about change management 17
        1.2.2   It's all about data 18
        1.2.3   Templates facilitate the start 19
        1.2.4   What does the basic data model look like 20
    1.3   Phase 2: Proactive-situational business analytics 22
        1.3.1   Dashboards as a success factor for DDM 22
        1.3.2   Customer data are essential for DDM 24
        1.3.3   Connecting internal and external data 25
        1.3.4   Using the value chain to reach the relevant market 26
    1.4   Phase 3: Interactive-dynamic business intelligence 27
    1.5   Phase 4: Dynamic Modeling Predictive Intelligence 28
    1.6   What is the decisive success factor 29
    Further reading 29

2 The conceptual ecosystem of DDM 31
    2.1   A/B tests 31
    2.2   Artificial Intelligence (AI) 32
    2.3   Artificial Neural Network (ANN) 32
    2.4   Reinforcement learning 32
    2.5   Evaluation metrics 32
    2.6   Big Data 33
    2.7   Business analysis vs. business analytics 33
    2.8   Business Intelligence (BI) 33
    2.9   Cloud Analytics 34
    2.10   Cloud-based social media analytics (CSMA) 34
    2.11   Cloud sourcing 34
    2.12   Clustering 35
    2.13   Data analysis 35
    2.14   Data Cleansing 35
    2.15   Data Lake 35
    2.16   Data mining 36

2.17 Data Science 36
2.18 Data Scientist..36
2.19 Deep Learning 36
2.20 Descriptive analytics...37
2.21 Descriptive analysis 37
2.22 Descriptive models 37
2.23 Exception Reporting 37
2.24 Extrapolation...37
2.25 Functional models or modeling 38
2.26 Hadoop cluster 38
2.27 Harvesting...38
2.28 Principal component analysis (PCA)..38
2.29 In-Sample..38
2.30 k-Means clustering..39
2.31 *k-nearest* neighbors..39
2.32 Classification 39
2.33 Louvain method 40
2.34 Machine learning 40
2.35 Feature extraction 40
2.36 Modeling...41
2.37 Model monitoring 41
2.38 Sample units..41
2.39 Neural networks..41
2.40 Out-of-Sample 42
2.41 Parameter..42
2.42 Predictive analysis 42
2.43 Predictive models or modeling 42
2.44 Predictors 43
2.45 Prescriptive analytics 43
2.46 Predictive marketing 43
2.47 Procurement Intelligence 44
2.48 Random Forrest 44
2.49 Regression analysis...45
2.50 Regularization...45
2.51 Training patterns 45
2.52 Unsupervised learning 45
2.53 Supervised learning 45
2.54 Validation 46
2.55 Variables...46
2.56 The dynamics of the DDM conceptual world..46
Further reading 47

3 The DDM Self-Assessment..49
3.1 The dimensions of the DDM assessment..49
3.1.1 The potential index 50
3.1.2 The value chain index..51

	3.1.3 The cost efficiency index	53
	3.1.4 The structure index	53
	3.1.5 The strategy index	53
	3.1.6 The distribution index	55
	3.1.7 The infrastructure index	55
	3.1.8 The competence index	56
3.2	The evaluation of the DDM assessment	56
3.3	Knowing where you stand	59
Further reading		61

Summary and Outlook **63**

Additional literature **67**

About the authors

Prof. h.c. Dr. Uwe Seebacher (MBA), who holds a doctorate in economics and business administration, has more than 25 years of experience as a consultant, manager but also entrepreneur in the media, production and service industries with international successes in strategic and operational marketing and communications as well as in process optimization, digitalization, human resources management and organizational development.

He is a lecturer at many renowned business schools and universities and has authored articles and books in many leading publishing houses, such as "Predictive Intelligence for Data-driven Managers" (Springer 2021), "B2B Marketing Guidebook" (Springer 2021), "Marketing Resource Management" (AQPS 2021), "Leadership Development" (Linde 2006) or "Template-based Management (Springer 2020).

For his innovative marketing concepts and initiatives, e.g., with Allianz, the European Union, the Austrian Federal Economic Chamber, Bayer Leverkusen and BASF, he received various awards, such as the Diskobolos Innovation Award of the European Chamber of Commerce and the 2016 Export Award of the Austrian Federal Economic Chamber. For more information, visit www.uweseebacher.org.

Julian Garritz has a degree in History from the National Autonomous University of Mexico. He is Founder and CEO of Garritz International, a digital agency and consulting firm with presence in Latin America, the United States and Europe. Leading the group's strategy from Frankfurt, Germany, he has successfully developed an international network that serves clients in different segments, including financial services, entertainment, health and industrial businesses.

Since 1998, he has worked in the development of digital projects, focusing on technology development and efficiency in communication, digital marketing and digital media buying. It currently has an international team of developers, data scientists, creatives and experts in digital media planning and buying with presence in Mexico City, Frankfurt, Panama City, New York and Coimbatore, India. In the context of B2B marketing, throughout his career he has worked with major brands of services, machinery and industrial products in Latin America, Europe and Asia. In 2013 he won a Gold Effie award for a recognized brand of choco-lates in Mexico for its digital strategy and sales generation. In 2018 he was awarded funding under the Löwe program by the government of the German state of Hessen for a project with the Frankfurt University Clinic dedicated to automation processes in the recognition and diagnosis of lung cancer in CT scans. In 2020, he and thyssenkrupp In-dustrial Solutions won the German Brand Award (Brand digitalization) for the development and execution of the digital advertising campaign for the presentation of mining machinery at the three-yearly BAUMA trade fair in Munich, Germany.

The procedure model for DDM

This chapter provides a compact overview and introductory presentation of the procedure for establishing data-driven management (DDM). It describes how DDM can be established in an organization step by step.

1.1 The maturity model to DDM

The maturity model for DDM (Fig. 1.1) was developed on the basis of various implementation projects in companies. The model comprises four levels. The model was developed in the course of expert interviews and on the basis of evaluations of various scientific papers, following the model for predictive intelligence (Seebacher 2021).

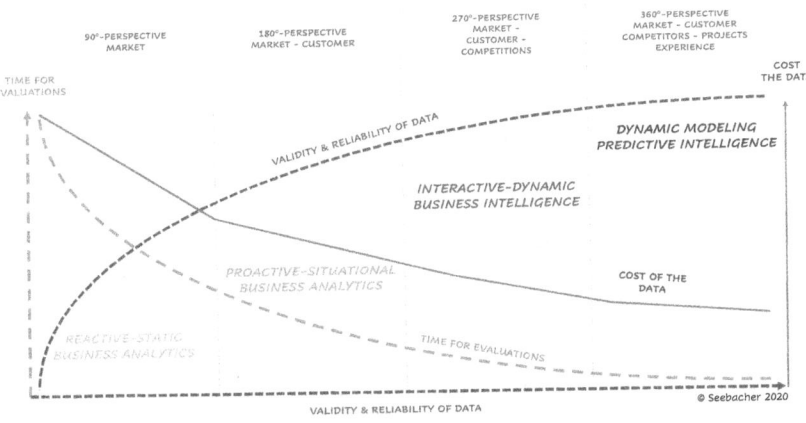

Fig. 1.1 Maturity model for DDM based on Seebacher 2021

The model looks schematically over time at the developments of the various relevant dimensions under consideration:

- Data costs
- Data quality
- Data evaluation time

The model divides the development into four levels or characteristics of how data is handled in organizations. The starting point, where about 95% of all companies still are today, is called *reactive-static business analytics*. This stage is characterized by high costs for data, long waiting times, and low validity and reliability with respect to data. In most cases, required analyses and studies are commissioned externally, which are used once and then do not flow to any further processing in the companies.

Development level 2 is referred to as *proactive-situational business analytics* (BA). At this level, BA is already used proactively in relation to specific management topics. This requires data to be available, validated and prepared in the organizations, but also maintained.

The third development stage goes hand in hand with an already 270° comprehensive data perspective and enables *interactive-dynamic business intelligence*. Operationally, this means that the department responsible for DDM must be continuously involved in all operational and strategic activities of the company management. As a result, an intensive exchange with the various internal departments has developed, for sound and profit-optimized corporate management.

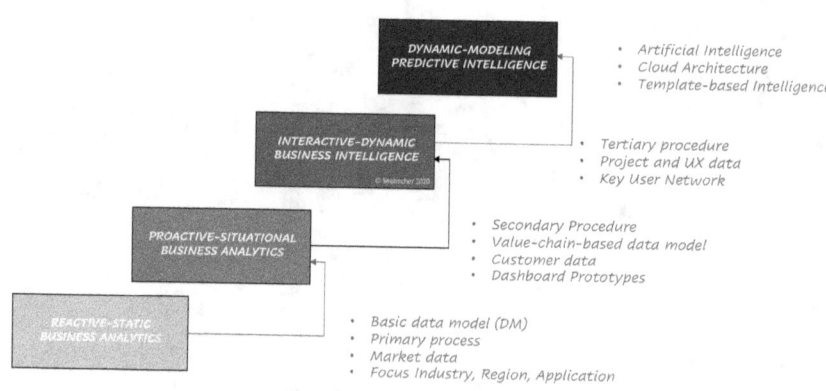

Fig. 1.2 Process model for DDM (Source: own representation based on Seebacher 2021)

Dynamic modeling predictive intelligence is the highest level of DDM and dynamically combines all relevant internal and external data dimensions into a 360° view in terms of content. The decisive difference to the other development levels is the competence of *interpretative* and *inferential* intelligence. This not only provides analyses and evaluations, but also enables concrete future simulations through the integration of self-learning applications, instruments and technologies in the sense of not only a statement about the probability of occurrence of future events, but also their applied operational design.

Based on this model for the development of DDM, the schematic process model for DDM was developed for this publication following Seebacher (2021) (Fig. 1.2). Based on the model, the most important activity areas for each stage of the development model can be derived, which must be carried out in order to move to the next maturity stage.

1.2 Phase 1: Reactive-static business analytics

Completing the first stage of DDM involves three core activities:

- Definition of important segments in relation to the respective organization to narrow down the initial relevant set of data to start with this selected data segment
- Selection of valid external providers of market and economic data and, based on this, structured collection and processing of this data for the internal servicing of research requests
- Definition and development of a basic data model with the help of which initial evaluations and analyses can be carried out

These activities can be designed and started without additional financial resources. This is a crucial aspect, because very few executives would allocate ex ante budgets and resources to a new, little-known topic, especially in the context of the fact that there is demonstrably little awareness of the high and strongly increasing relevance of data in today's top management. Therefore, the entire process model presented here is designed to realize and thus communicate tangible successes within a short period of time without additional costs, in order to be able to expand and extend the DDM activities step by step as a result - always jointly and in close coordination with the entire organization.

1.2.1 It's all about change management

Classic change management theory proves that the willingness to change is greatest when there are problems, such as being behind plan in terms of sales. In the context of the first phase, this means that one should look for such problem areas within the organization. To find such areas, it is necessary to look structurally at the sales figures of the respective organization. How can this be implemented operationally? The concrete approach depends on the size but also the geographical presence of the respective organization. The following criteria are relevant:

- Number of countries or regions relevant to sales and marketing
- Number of industries served

Based on these two categories, the following four scenarios can be defined for guidance:

- Scenario 1: National organization with one product or industry
- Scenario 2: Regional or international organization with one product or industry
- Scenario 3: National organization with several products and / or with focus on several industries
- Scenario 4: Regional or international organization with multiple products and / or with focus on multiple industries

For all scenarios, the basic rule is that you have to create access to sales. Initially, it is crucial to assume that you will immediately encounter headwinds if you bring the wrong person on board. It is always a matter of organizational sovereignty and sensitivities. During the entire DDM setup work, it is therefore important to ensure that the standard distribution for readiness for change is taken into account, with 20% willing to change, 60% neutral to change, and 20% change resisters. Therefore, consider who in sales or even in finance can be classified as trustworthy. Approach this person and make an appointment. The content of this first meeting should be a reflection discussion on how to work even better with DDM for the benefit of the entire company.

During the first exchange, the possibilities of modern marketing will be presented. It is about selected topics of modern (B2B) marketing such as LinkedIn - focus campaigns, social selling or but also lead scanning, lead nurturing (Seebacher 2020). On the basis of these topics, it will be explained how efficiently and effectively sales can be supported in a very targeted manner on the basis of the latest, cost-minimizing technologies. Against this background, it should then be critically discussed and debated together in which area of sales it would be useful and just necessary to support. In every organization, there are always certain sales areas where there is room for improvement. This or these must be identified, because the relevant product manager or the responsible sales employee will in any case be interested in doing everything possible to optimize a weakening turnover.

1.2.2 It is about data

Once the first pilot customers have been identified in terms of data and sales, the next step is to compile the necessary information and data material. An overview of always up-to-date database providers is provided by many different, freely accessible institutions, such as the Vienna University of Economics and Business, whose overview can be accessed via the following QRC (Fig. 1.3).

Fig. 1.3 QRC to WU Vienna for retrieving database providers (Source: own representation)

However, the European Commission also provides an overview of relevant economic databases that are freely accessible at the following link (Fig. 1.4).

Fig. 1.4 QRC to the European Commission for retrieving economic databases (source: own representation)

These are just two of many different websites that provide an overview of relevant business databases. Seebacher (2021) provides a comprehensive overview of the most common and renowned databases broken down by industry.

1.2.3 Templates facilitate the start

Especially at the beginning of DDM activities, it is crucial not to leave anything to chance. The path to DDM is like a paradigm shift and an enormous organizational learning process. The goal must be to be able to process more and more requests for analyses, evaluations and research internally efficiently and effectively. This requires the entire process to be stringent and goal-oriented, so that there are as few loops and repetitions as possible. Following the work on template-based management (Seebacher 2020), the instrument of templates can be used.

If you set up a simple, standardized and, for example, MS Excel-based inquiry monitoring system with regard to the incoming research requests, then it is possible to plan well by when the various analyses, elaborations and reports can be completed internally. At this point, clean communication again comes into play as part of expectation management. After receiving the request, an e-mail is immediately returned with the reference that the request has been received and documented. The template (Fig. 1.5) for specifying the search request is automatically attached to this e-mail in order to be able to query the requirements efficiently and effectively.

Date (dd.mm.yyyy)	
Submitted by (Function & Name)	
Internal contact person(s) for data validation, if different from the applicant	
Deadline (by what date should the data be delivered - e.g. for a specific event that is about to happen)	
Capex and/or Opex	
Industry (specify one or more)	
Request (if relevant; optional: specific process step)	
Business decision to be made or business basis for the request *To avoid redundancies	
Scope of the data to be retrieved *please specify as detailed as possible e.g.: geographical scope, specific technologies, sub-applications, relevant time period (timeframe), required future prospects, external and/or internal data such as from CRM, customs tariff numbers, tender identification numbers, etc.	
Required format of the work to be delivered (PPT, Excel)	

Fig. 1.5 Template for submitting a search request (source: own representation)

With the help of this template, the time for defining queries can be significantly minimized. On the other hand, the template protects the DDM team, which thus does not have to process requests that are not sufficiently and validly defined.

1.2.4 What does the basic data model look like

In addition to clear processes and templates, the data model underlying a future in-house DDM environment is the most important and, in the long run, the all-important element. Such a data model must be carefully designed, structured and developed step by step. It is the core on which everything else is ultimately built. Each additional datum must be able to be integrated into the existing DDM data model and linked to it.

In addition, the initially static, temporally one-dimensional data model must subsequently be able to work and calculate in a temporally multidimensional, dynamically regressive, but also extrapolative manner. For this purpose, the company's own algorithms must be integrated into the data model or stored in it. Although, from a structural point of view, existing data structures and mechanisms are of course always used, a DDM environment can only generate maximum added value in the long term without compromise if no generic mechanisms are used, but mechanisms that are adapted and adapted specifically to the needs of the target organization.

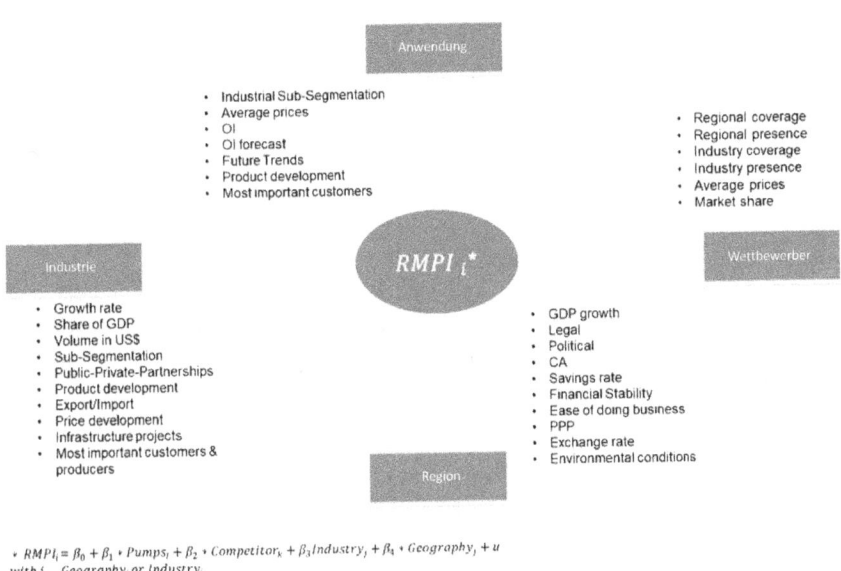

• $RMPI_i = \beta_0 + \beta_1 \cdot Pumps_i + \beta_2 \cdot Competitor_k + \beta_3 Industry_j + \beta_4 \cdot Geography_l + u$
with $i ... Geography_i$ or $Industry_i$

Fig. 1.6 Schematic representation of a DDM base data model (Source: Seebacher 2021).

This requires that such a data model is developed step by step from scratch and is continuously refined and extended. The basic model for DDM contains four essential areas (Fig. 1.6):

- Application or segment data
- Industry data
- Geographical economic data
- Competitor data

With this Excel-based data model, initial evaluations and analyses can be realized. These initial results are still pulled manually from the Excel tableau, in order to be subsequently incorporated into a PowerPoint documentation that can be presented. Normally, such analyses and reports will comprise between 10 and 20 pages and will immediately enable the internal customer to solve the respective task.

1.3 Phase 2: Proactive-situational business analytics

After about six to 12 months, the step towards phase 2 should happen. The time span is not the decisive criterion here, but the *authenticity of implementation*. This refers to the penetration of the organization as well as the arrival of the topic in the organization. Ultimately, this is a drastic change process. The entire structural elements described above are only the enablers and drivers of this paradigmatic, organizational realignment, because they will only be used sustainably and meaningfully if the mindset and the indisputable necessity of such a type of corporate management also really arrive in the minds of the acting persons.

1.3.1 Dashboards as a success factor for DDM

Once the basic data model for DDM is established and available, an enormous portfolio of graphics and charts on markets and industries will be generated and thus available after a short time.

This automatically leads to the desire not to have to create separate, manually generated graphics and overviews for each research request, because this means an unnecessary amount of time and, in addition, the stringency and consistency also suffers. So, this automation but also the subsequent replicability will happen on its own. In the beginning, for the sake of simplicity, it will be MS Excel overviews that depict different data areas by default in order to provide a clearly structured overview at a glance. An initial overview of this kind can include the following five areas, for example (Fig. 1.7):

- Selection area with filters for continents, regions and individual countries, in order to be able to adapt the contents of the other four areas or to narrow them down to the respective needs
- General market data
- Socioeconomic data
- Economic data
- Trade statistics

Building on this, the market data area (Fig. 1.8) can in turn contain its own filter area (1) to filter out a specific industry (2) for a region or country, for example, which is then displayed in the form of the entire (light) but also relevant (dark)

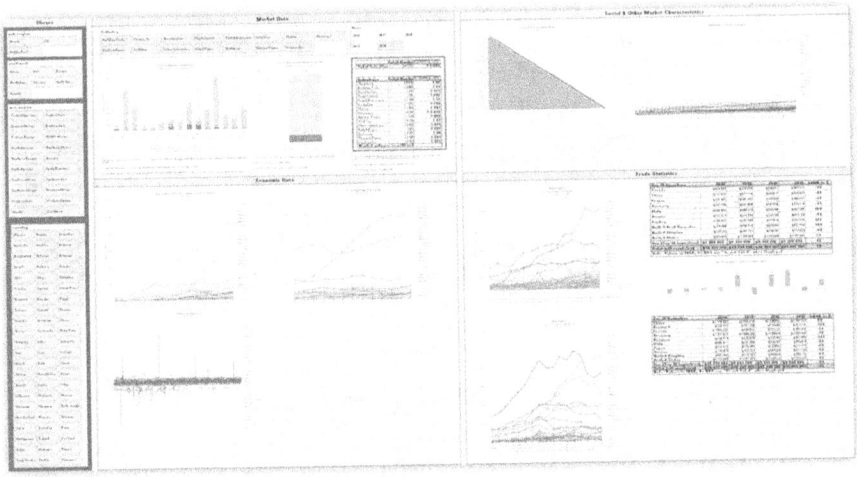

Fig. 1.7 Dashboard prototype (source: own representation)

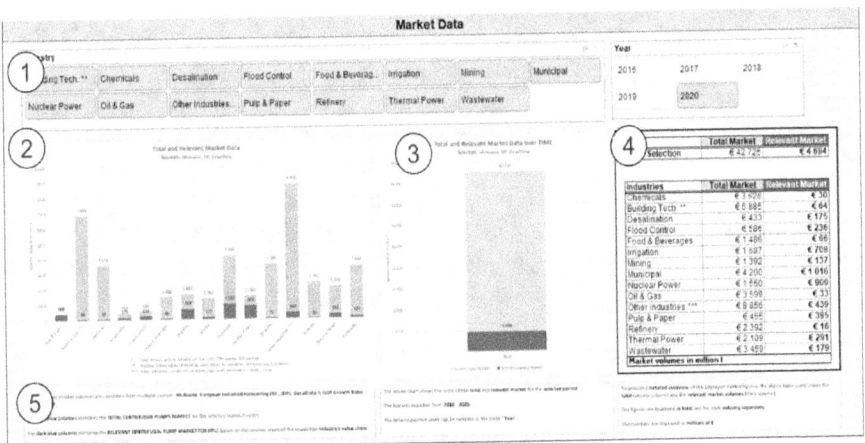

Fig. 1.8 Area market data from Excel-based dashboard prototype (Source: Seebacher 2021)

market (3) and is also displayed numerically with a mouse-over function[1]. Tabular areas (4) are suitable for improving the user experience (UX), which in turn depict the graphical comparison (2) in figures. Additional information and explanations can be mapped in separate meta-data areas (5) and therefore minimize queries and interpretation possibilities. Many other DDM dashboard templates can be found in

---

[1] https://de.wikipedia.org/wiki/Tooltip. Accessed: April 13, 2021

Seebacher (2021), which also provides a good overview of the many different options for data preparation along the DDM development process.

> Tip: If the organization in question has a corresponding corporate design specification, this should not be ignored from the outset. Even if MS Excel is not the paradigm tool for sophisticated, "award-worthy" designs, it offers sufficient scope for at least color compliance with existing corporate design specifications.

1.3.2 The customer data are essential for DDM

The next step is to extend the data model to include customer data. Once again, it is advisable to start small. If the company does not have a system in which customer-relevant data is recorded, it is possible to start collecting initial customer data simply and pragmatically on the basis of MS Excel. With regard to the approach of looking for where the shoe pinches in terms of sales, one can approach a relevant colleague and offer assistance. A first step can be a simple customer survey to evaluate indications of possible optimization potential in terms of processes or products. The result can be easily evaluated and processed and represents the first quick win. This should show added value in the context of DDM for the first time and be brought to the attention of management accordingly.

If a CRM is in place, it is recommended to pull data on specific customers or products from the CRM. This requires access to the CRM system, which may or may not be available depending on the organizational unit in which one is located. In this context, the following initial scenarios can again be derived:

- Scenario 1: CRM does not exist in the organization
- Scenario 2: CRM already exists in the organization
    - Scenario 2.1: Access to the CRM system is not available
    - Scenario 2.2: Access to the CRM system is available

Scenario 2.2 is ideal, of course, because then everything that is needed is available. So you can get started and pull data in a structured way for the first time, or fetch data from the CRM in relation to the search queries to be processed on a situational basis, in order to be able to recognize what data is actually available in the CRM system and what is not.

> Tip: At this point, it is worth pointing out the biggest pitfall with regard to the CRM system (Seebacher 2020). The term CRM is often used without differentiating between the content and technical dimensions of the term or system. This often leads to discussions about the sovereignty of the CRM. By no means is the technical sovereignty over the CRM within the framework of the

DDM intended or wanted, but the content-related work with data will inevitably go hand in hand with a deeper qualitative examination of the CRM content. This will identify content-related shoals and fuzziness, but also opportunities for optimizing data quality and user-friendliness, which should then be implemented in the sense of sustainable predictive intelligence in coordination with the various stakeholders.

1.3.3 Connect internal and external data

The connection of external data with internal data opens up a completely new dimension of viewing. Because suddenly, cause-effect relationships can be enabled, evaluated and then discussed. Product flows (Fig. 1.9) can be extracted in relation to certain applications or industries, which in turn makes it possible to analyze why a product sells disproportionately in relation to an application and the relevant market potential. This circumstance in turn provides new insights into product characteristics, which can be further optimized in a targeted manner and then actively marketed for other applications as a previously unknown *Unique Selling Proposition* (USP).

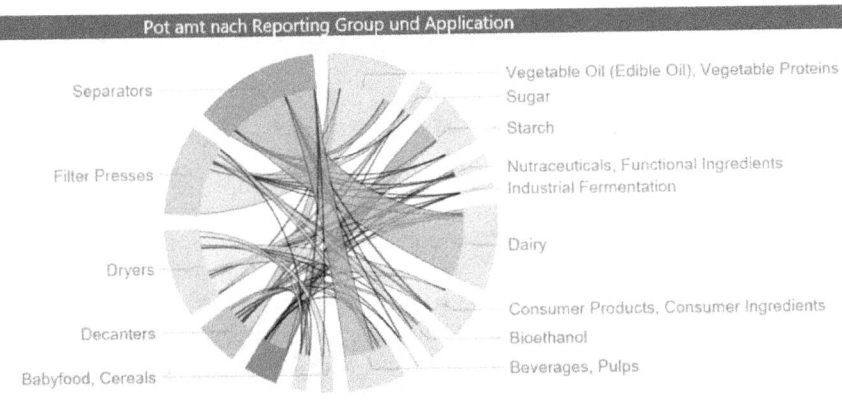

Fig. 1.9 DDM product flow analysis from external and internal data (source: Seebacher 2021).

On the other hand, more complex convergence evaluations can be created in terms of absolute and relevant markets and the corresponding proportionalities (Fig. 1.10). All these charts are only examples, because with step-by-step DDM realization, many more creative and situation-specific, value-added views and evaluations will emerge together with colleagues. At the granular level, everything revolves around data fields and records that must be connected by a criterion in a multidimensional data cube (MDW). This means that it is not necessary to always transfer an entire data set, but just individual components from it. If this is not taken into account, the MDW is unnecessarily inflated, which in turn affects the performance of the MDW and thus the user-friendliness.

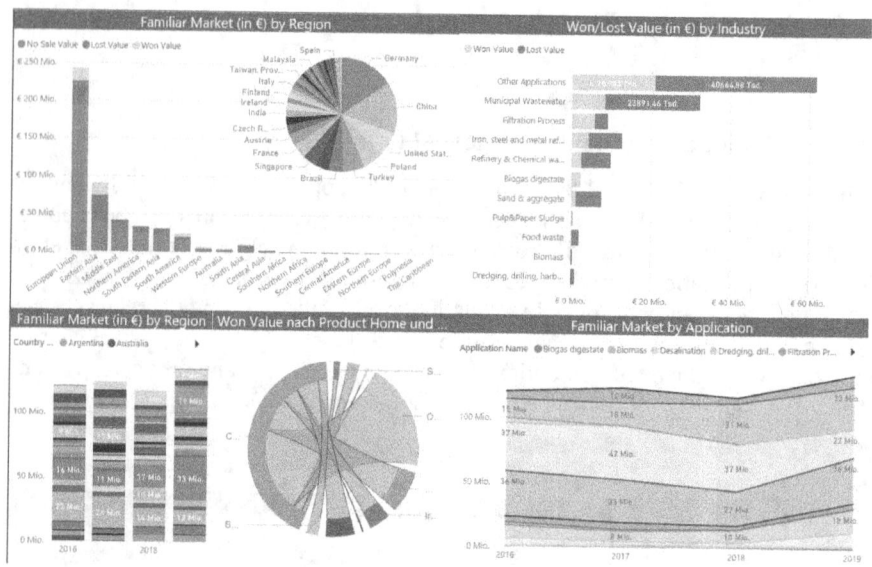

Fig. 1.10 Customer market data dashboard (source: Seebacher 2021)

1.3.4 With the value chain to the relevant market

Another important step on the second stage of the DDM development model is the integration of the value creation view. The aim is to identify which part of an industrial value chain one can cover as a company with the respective current product portfolio.

Statistics show that 80 percent of companies can only cover between 10 and 30 percent of an industrial value chain. However, if data on entire industries is used in the context of the DDM, this results in a completely false picture, as the *absolute market differs* significantly from the *market* that *is relevant for* a company, namely the one for which the respective company also has the products in its portfolio. Thus, the distinction between the absolute and relevant market is essential with regard to the validity and precision of the data. The goal must therefore be to use the value-added analysis to extract the relevant market for one's own company from the respective absolute market and to integrate this into the DDM data model. A detailed procedure and various case studies in this context can be found in Seebacher (2021).

1.4 Phase 3: Interactive-dynamic business intelligence

When the third stage of the maturity model is reached, the comprehensive and significant added value of data-driven corporate management slowly and gradually becomes more and more transparent. It is now a matter of being able to devote more attention to the conceptual work in the context of data-driven corporate management and development. It is therefore necessary to focus on the following three areas of activity within the framework of the third level of the DDM:

- Key User Network (KUN)
- Integration of project data and data on customer experience (CX) or user experience (UX) (Halb and Seebacher 2020)
- Expansion of activities to include tertiary analyses

A *key user network* (KUN) can be defined and set up very quickly and very effectively. The following steps have to be gone through in order to benefit from this powerful concept in a timely manner:

- Define criteria for key users (KU)
- Create description of DDM-KUN including goals, benefits and tasks.
- Identify and contact KU
- Define training content for KU or KUN members
- Produce training content in the form of eLearning , podcasts or webinars
- Implement trainings
- Activate KUN and keep it informed

In addition to the ongoing further development of the interactive views and designs, the remaining data gaps - data on projects, key customers and the customer experience - must also be closed. The area of projects predominantly targets organizations that have to deal with long lead times, even in the area of large tenders and major projects. For such organizations, it is and can be of enormous importance to also have this information in the DDM environment in order to always be up to date and also, under the aspect of account-based marketing (ABM) (Bacon 2020), to be able to provide corresponding and involved organizations and their information-seeking employees with information in the best possible way on the respective right media and channels.

In addition to the project data, the social breadcrumbs of prospects and customers should also be integrated into the DDM data model at this stage at the latest. In this way, the 360° all-round view can be achieved, and this information can be integrated into the overall analytics. This information is essential, on the one hand, to be able to conclude the urgency of a possible investment based on the activity level and, on the other hand, to see which content is consumed for how long and via which channel through the so-called *Interesting Moments*. These evaluations not only enable sales to recognize where they should be active, but also make it clear to marketing which content performs better in which form at which time of day in which region via which channel and which performs less well.

1.5 Phase 4: Dynamic Modeling Predictive Intelligence

To start with, the most difficult part has already been successfully mastered when this fourth stage is reached, because now only the free skating remains. For this, however, it is essential to have fully understood and internalized the steps and activities described above, because the activities that lie ahead now require comprehensive expertise in all existing PI structures, processes and connections. In concrete terms, we are now dealing with three areas:

- Extension of the DDM environment with Template-based Intelligence (TBI)
- Realization or validation of a DDM cloud architecture
- Integration of Artificial Intelligence (AI) into the DDM Environment

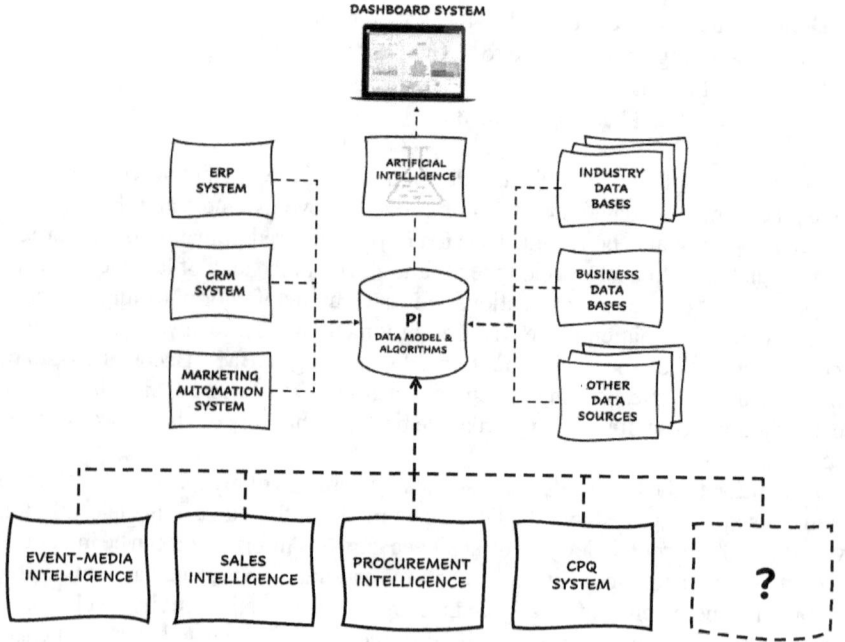

Fig. 1.11 DDM-IT blueprint (source: Seebacher 2021)

Continuing the increasing automation of DDM workflows, more extensive tasks can now be gradually outsourced to internal customers at this level of the DDM maturity model using template-based intelligence. Template-based intelligence (TBI) is based on the template-based management (TBM) approach (Seebacher 2020) and enables, for example, the automated creation or generation of a comprehensive economic analysis in the form of a DDM -supported workflow.

TBI can be used for the following use cases, among others:

- Market entry studies
- Product diversification analyses
- *Dynamic pricing* analyses
- Innovation Management Program Planning
- *Procurement intelligence* calculations
- Product launch planning
- R&D program planning

In addition, the now very advanced DDM data model and data system should be placed on a solid information technology basis. This should also be done against the background that the potential of artificial intelligence should also be used at the latest at this point in time. Figure 1.11 shows an overview of a reasonable sustainable IT environment for data-driven management (Seebacher 2021). This infrastructure can be developed and emerge gradually over time without significant investment.

1.6 What is the decisive success factor

Success is the result of many small steps. This is also and especially true for the field of data-driven management. Only those organizations will profit efficiently and effectively from DDM in the long term that also manage to launch DDM authentically and organically in their own organization. This means that the decisive development of competence must take place within the organization and must be wanted and driven forward by it. Otherwise, we run the risk of experiencing a development similar to that in the context of CRM systems, which to this day do not have the corresponding acceptance in most companies, but also do not deliver the corresponding added value.

Further reading

Bacon, A. (2020). *Account-based marketing*. In U. Seebacher (Hrsg.), B2B marketing - A guidebook for the classroom to the boardroom. Cham: Springer.

Ermer, B. (2020). *Social Selling im B2B Marketing*. In U. Seebacher (Ed.), B2B marketing - A guidebook for the classroom to the boardroom. Cham: Springer.

Halb, F., & Seebacher, U. (2020). *Customer experience und touchpoint management*. In U. Seebacher (Hrsg.), B2B Marketing - A guidebook for the classroom to the boardroom. New York: Springer.

Scheer, P., & Kasper, H. (2011). *Leadership and social competence*. Munich: Linde Verlag.

Seebacher, U. (2020a). *B2B marketing - A guidebook for the classroom to the boardroom*. Cham: Springer.

Seebacher, U. (2020b). *B2B marketing essential: How to turn your marketing from a cost into a sales engine* (2nd ed.). Graz: AQPS.

Seebacher, U. (2020c). *Template-based management - A guide for an efficient and impactful professional practice*. Cham: Springer.

Seebacher, U. (2021). *Predictive intelligence for managers: the easy way to data-driven business management - with self-assessment, procedure model and case studies*. Heidelberg: Springer.

Sturm, A., Opferbeck, I., & Gurt, J. (2011). *Organizational psychology*. Wiesbaden: VS Verlag für Sozialwissenschaften.

2 The conceptual ecosystem of DDM

In this section, the most essential expressions in the environment of DDM are cited and simply described. The subject area is subject to demanding dynamics, so this overview must be considered a snapshot. The attempt is made to focus on per se established and widely used expressions and not to mention those that are used selectively in the context of such a listing for the sake of a general overview.

Data-driven management has evolved from the term *Business Intelligence in order* to meet the need to not only evaluate facts in a forward-looking manner, but instead to implicitly relate them just as directly to concrete management decisions - in the sense of valid recommendations for decisions and actions. The term "Business Intelligence" was developed by the consulting firm *Gartner in* 1989 and has since become firmly established in the innovative management vocabulary. Business Intelligence (BI) refers to the techniques, processes and skills needed to collect and analyze information and transform data into actionable insights and information.

In recent years, the terminology around *business analytics has* also emerged, resulting in the interchangeable and confusing use of these and similar terms. The increasing popularity of those and similar expressions can be attributed to the rapid developments in the field of analysis of facts related to, for example, *in-memory, advanced algorithms, artificial intelligence* (AI) or *machine learning,* etc., which have massively increased the performance of business intelligence software. More and more and modern expressions in the subject area of modern business management do not contribute in every case to a compellingly better comprehensibility and make it more difficult for the top management to make and initiate the adequate, necessary decisions for the respective own company.

English and German terms are sometimes used in the chapter. This selection was made in relation to the frequency of use of the terms in order to show the reader the more common term in this list.

2.1 A/B tests

This procedure describes the comparison and testing of different measures or options for action by exchanging and changing individual components, characteristics, criteria or parameters. The procedure plays a decisive role in the context of resource allocation.

2.2 Artificial Intelligence (AI)

Artificial Intelligence (AI) originated in the field of computer science and is therefore also a branch of computer science. AI deals with the automation of intelligent behavior and the learning of machines, machine learning, as this will be defined later. An exact delimitation or definition of the term would require a precise definition of "intelligence" as a basis, which, however, does not exist.

Neural networks can be considered the forerunners of today's AI, as they replicate the philanthropic brain and map it in the computer to replicate the functioning of the human brain. The ever more rapid development in the performance of PCs allows such artificial networks to become more and more powerful and to achieve a learning ability similar to that of the brain. When artificial intelligence surpasses human intelligence, the state of the Technological Singularity will be reached.

In relation to data-driven management, the category of AI will play an increasingly important role. Only with the help of the integration of AI can DDM calculate more precisely the effects of an alternative course of action within the framework of corporate management, extrapolate this relationally and then constructively identify new parameters that change with this or develop to the disadvantage.

2.3 Artificial Neural Network (ANN)

Artificial neural networks (KNN) are networks of artificial neurons. They are the subject of research in neuroinformatics and represent a branch of artificial intelligence. KNNs and ANNs are becoming increasingly important in data-driven management, as they are able to make increasingly precise predictions. In the majority of cases, KNNs are based on the interconnection of many McCulloch-Pitts neurons or light versions of them, such as the high-order neuron. The topology of a network in terms of the assignment of links and nodes must be structured depending on the defined project objective in order to be able to generate knowledge with surplus from Big Data.

2.4 Reinforcement learning

In contrast to unsupervised and supervised learning, where the packages once implemented continue to be used unchanged, in reinforcement learning a model constantly novellates itself beyond this by rapidly incorporating the generated solutions as feedback into the model from scratch.

2.5 Evaluation metrics

Once the model is defined and implemented, the accuracy of the model must be evaluated based on model predictions, namely Predictive Intelligence Precision (PIP). This means that basic PI methods are compared to determine which of several different methods can be used to generate the best prediction for the situation or problem defined. The three most common evaluation indicators are:

- Classification indicators: This category includes the percentage of correct predictions (as the simplest evaluation method) and the so-called truth matrix or confusion matrix.
- Regression Metric: The root mean square determines the prediction error as the difference between the predicted value and the actual value.

2.6 Big Data

This term originates from the English world and broadly refers to data that is too large, too complex, too fast or too weak to be analyzed using manual and conventional data processing methods (Christl 2014). In the narrowest sense, Big Data refers to the processing of large, complex, and rapidly changing amounts of data. In the narrowest sense, the term refers to a precisely defined type of data, and "big" refers to the four dimensions

- volume (scope, data volume),
- *velocity* (speed at which the data volumes are generated and transferred),
- *variety* (range of data types and sources) and
- veracity (authenticity of data).

2.7 Business analysis vs. business analytics

Based on the similarity of terms such as business analysis and business analytics, it becomes clear and understandable to define the importance and meaning of related and used technical terms. The purpose of business analysis (BA) is to understand the structures and process of a business (IIBA® International Institute of Business Analysis 2017). Suggested actions and recommendations are made that enable the organization to address deficiencies in the structure and process organization. Examples include optimized workflows, organizational changes and, in particular, the use of IT tools.

Business analytics is based on the so-called data optimization process. It is a strategic tool for modern business management and control. As an important aspect of data-driven management, its purpose is not only to provide answers to the question "What was in the past?", but also "What will it be in the future?".

2.8 Business Intelligence (BI)

The definition of Business Intelligence (BI) is the process of collecting, processing and providing data for decision making (Chamoni and Gluchowski 2006). In the context of business management, it tends to be based on standard instructions with consistent key indicators for measurement and analysis. As part of business intelligence, a consistent, predefined reporting structure should be used to answer predefined questions based on dashboards. This can be achieved through indirect access or manual, or partially or fully automated multi-dimensional data sources, database and system aggregation.

2.9 Cloud Analytics

This term describes a service model in which part of the data analysis is performed in a public or private cloud and results are obtained from it. In most cases, cloud analytics applications offer usage-based pricing models. The connection between companies and users via the Internet is changing cloud analytics in terms of the labor market economy.

Therefore, cloud analytics refers to all analytics processes in which one or more of the elements are implemented or will be implemented in the cloud. Examples of cloud analytics products and services include hosted data warehouses, SaaS BI (software as a service business intelligence), and cloud-based social media analytics. Currently, Amazon's Mechanical Turk or oDesk are the most widely used systems in this area.

2.10 Cloud-based Social Media Analytics (CSMA)

Cloud-based social media analytics involves the use of various tools to not only identify the best platform and site for a defined task or target, but also to identify individual applications for data transfer, capture, storage services, and data analytics software.

2.11 Cloud sourcing

This term consists of *cloud computing* and *outsourcing*, which define the external procurement of IT services, data and solutions from the cloud environment. In fact, cloud sourcing is an important part of today's hybrid IT procurement strategy. One can compare cloud sourcing with outsourcing. However, nowadays the cost of cloud soucring services is mainly based on a usage model (pay-per-use) rather than on an annual or monthly contract. In the context of DDM, the term refers to which applications, data, tools or functions are to be acquired from outside. The aspects to be considered are security, performance, cost and the IT strategy of the respective company. Therefore, it can be systematically defined and optimally used over a long period of time by appropriately combining internal and external hardware and software elements.

2.12 Clustering

Clustering, a cluster analysis, refers to a procedure for identifying groups using a so-called clustering algorithm. Some publications also use the term aggregation analysis, which is derived from a graphical representation, where the result can be an aggregation of one or more data points. This is the process of finding similar structures in large databases. Groups of "similar" objects found in this way are called clusters, and group assignments are called clusters. The similarity group found can be graph theory, stratification, partitioning or optimization.

2.13 Data analysis

Data analysis uses statistical methods to generate value-added information from data. Three different models of data analysis are distinguished:

- **Descriptive data analysis**: represent data from a sample or population using ratios or graphs.
- **Inferential data analysis** : Infer from the sample to the characteristics of the unsampled population.
- **Exploratory data analysis** : identify relationships between different variables.
- **Context-based data analysis** : identify constellations in content-related data.

2.14 Data Cleansing

Data cleansing is also referred to as *data editing*. An important process in this context is the identification of duplicate data records, which refers to the recognition and merging of the same data records - duplicates - and data fusion as the merging and completion of incomplete data. Data cleansing focuses on optimizing the quality of information.

Ideally, this is done at the beginning of actions in the context of DDM to ensure and be able to guarantee that the realized results and findings are valid and reliable.

2.15 Data Lake

Data lake refers to a large amount of raw data for which no use has yet been defined. The difference to the classic *data warehouse*[2] is that in such a data *warehouse* the data is structured and filtered for an already defined purpose or a specific task.

---

[2] https://en.wikipedia.org/wiki/Data_Warehouse. Accessed: April 12, 2021

2.16 Data mining

This term is used as an Anglicism, which is why there is no German term for this term yet. *Data mining* refers to the systematic application of the methods of classical statistics to large data sets. Data mining aims at determining new insights from the data sets with respect to correlations, cross-connections or trends. Due to their size, large data sets have to be processed computer aided. In recent years, data mining has increasingly become a subset of the broader process of *Knowledge Discovery in Databases (KDD)*,. While KDD also includes steps such as data cleansing and preprocessing as well as evaluation, data mining is limited to the actual processing step of the process itself (Fayyad et al. 1996).

2.17 Data Science

Data Science defines the extraction of knowledge from data (Dhar 2013) as an interdisciplinary science. The term has existed since the 1960s as a replacement for the term "computer science" and was first used freely by Peter Naur in 1974 in the Concise Survey of Computer Methods.

Every data science project must always include the following four steps: first, the data must be processed and prepared. Then the appropriate algorithms are selected, followed by parameter optimization of the algorithms. On this basis, models are then derived, from whose comparison - evaluation and validation - the best for the situation is then identified (Ng and Soo 2018).

2.18 Data Scientist

The job description of a data scientist is still a very young job description and corresponding training courses have only been offered very sporadically to date. Often, the training to become a data scientist is linked to an existing education in the field of economics, computer science or statistics, which has a positive effect on employability (Güpner 2015).

2.19 Deep Learning

Deep learning is the term used in current literature to describe *deep learning*. It is a machine learning method that uses artificial neural networks (KNN) (Borgelt et al. 2003). These KNNs are equipped with multiple layers, or *hidden layers,* between the input layer and the output layer, thereby defining an extensive internal structure. Deep Learning has only gained importance in the recent course of developments in artificial intelligence.

2.20 Descriptive analytics

Important in this context is the distinction between the terms analytics and analysis. The difference between analysis and analytics is that the science concerned with carrying out the analysis of a fact or an object is called analytics, in the figurative sense of a meta-analysis. Thus, the term descriptive analytics refers to a descriptive evaluation of fundamental analyses.

2.21 Descriptive analysis

Descriptive analysis falls within the subject area of descriptive statistics. Descriptive data analysis has an exclusively descriptive character, which is derived from the Latin word "describere" in the sense of "to describe".

2.22 Descriptive models

Descriptive models establish connections and relationships in defined data sets in terms of groupings and classifications. In contrast to predictive models, descriptive models are concerned with the recognition and identification of resilient dependencies, relationships and interrelationships. It is about identifying dependencies and interdependencies in order to be able to substantiate and represent possible questions of corporate management not only one-dimensionally, but multidimensionally on this basis.

2.23 Exception Reporting

Modern business intelligence infrastructures not only generate defined reports and aggregated data, but also enable the triggering of automated information provision when defined thresholds are reached or exceeded (Felden and Buder 2012, p. 17ff).

2.24 Extrapolation

This term refers to an extrapolation or determination of a mostly mathematical behavior, such as a series of numbers over a defined period of time, beyond the secured or existing (data) range. The following variants could be defined:

- Static extrapolation
- Dynamic extrapolation
- Monodimensional extrapolation
- Multidimensional extrapolation

2.25 Functional models or modeling

With the functional model, the focus is on transforming or changing the data. Functional models can also be integrated into operational applications and data products to provide real-time analysis capabilities.

2.26 Hadoop cluster

A *Hadoop cluster* is a coordinated linkage of hardware to achieve greater processing capacity of large, unstructured data sets. Hadoop clusters operate on a *master-slave model*, a model for a communication protocol in which one device or process, referred to as the *master,* controls one or more devices or processes, defined as *slaves*.

2.27 Harvesting

Harvesting in the context of data-driven management means *harvesting* data or information. The term *Information Harvesting* (IH) was established by Ralphe Wiggins (1992) as an attempt to derive rules from data sets. In this context, IH can also be seen as a form of machine learning and falls within the scope of today's *data mining* .

2.28 Principal component analysis (PCA)

This term refers to the method of identifying those variables by which data points can best be broken down. It is a dimensionality reduction method, as data can be described by a smaller set of variables, the principal components. Such principal components can also be understood as dimensions along which data points are most widely distributed (Fig. 2.1), where a principal component can be expressed by one or more variables. Each principal component represents a weighted sum of the original variables.

PCA as a method is best suited when the most informative dimensions have the greatest scatter in the data and are also perpendicular to all others.

2.29 In-Sample

This term refers to sample units or records that are directly related to a sample of data being processed. The opposite is defined by the term *out-of-sample.*

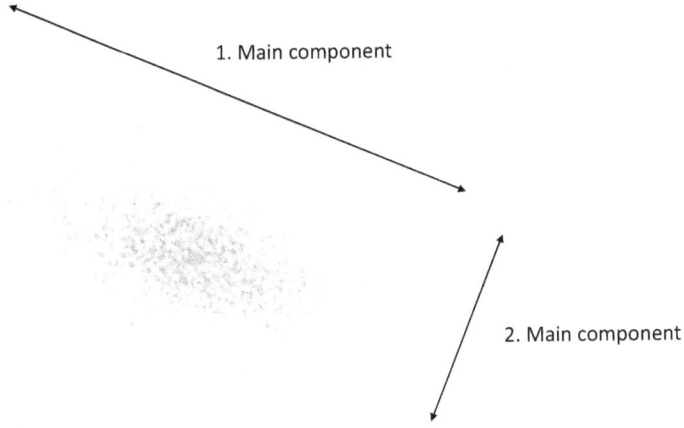

Fig. 2.1 Visualization of two main components (source: own representation)

2.30 k-Means clustering

This term defines a supervised learning technique. The technique groups similar data points into groups called clusters. In this context, k specifies how many groups are to be mapped.

2.31 k-nearest neighbors

This method is also often referred to as kNN or outlier detection. However, it should not be confused with KNN, Artificial Neural Networks. *k-nearest* neighbors (kNN) is an algorithm for classifying a data point based on the properties of its neighbors. The "k" itself is in turn a parameter representing the set of nearest neighbors used by the algorithm. Therefore, an optimal k value is that which associates the data points with a reasonable mean number of neighbors. Additionally, this method can also be used to predict continuous data values by aggregating the nearest neighbor values.

2.32 Classification

Technical terms such as *typification* or *systematics* are also used for the term classification. The aim is to establish an overview of objects ordered in a data set and to enable thematic search in order to develop an order. It is about a planned generation of abstract classes to enable a delimitation or to develop an order. In this context, the terms *classification* or *class assignment* refer to the application of a classification to an object by selecting an appropriate class of a defined, given classification. For the area of data-driven management, a distinction is made between *conceptual* classification, *deductive classification,* and *qualitative* classification.

2.33 Louvain method

This method is a procedure to detect clusters in a network. It goes back to a group of researchers led by Blondel et al. (2008) from the University of Louvain. The method tests different configurations of groupings to maximize the number and strength of edges between nodes in the same cluster and minimize the number and strength of edges between nodes in different clusters. The extent to which this criterion is met is called modularity, and the optimal assignment to a cluster is the one with the highest modularity.

2.34 Machine learning

Machine learning is a generic term for the generation of knowledge from experience using "artificial" methods. For this purpose, special algorithms are used to learn from large amounts of data, from Big Data. Appropriate statistical models are used, which are based on training data. Through the so-called learning transfer, these learning experiences can subsequently also be applied to unknown data and thus be subjected to an evaluation. If a machine fails on an unknown data set, the term overfitting is used for this.

Machine learning distinguishes between *symbolic* and *non-symbolic* approaches and *algorithmic* approaches, which in turn are divided into supervised and unsupervised learning. With regard to Data Driven Management, it is crucial to have machine learning in mind because, in the further course of development, the maturity model underlying Data Driven Management will in any case make this technology increasingly important.

2.35 Feature extraction

If suitable variables must first be drawn for a calculation, this is referred to as feature extraction. Not only can the values of a single variable be regrouped, but multiple variables can be grouped together, which is called dimension reduction. With this process, it is possible to draw the most interesting and useful information from a large number of variables and then analyze it using a smaller set of variables.

2.36 Modeling

Modeling is generally defined as the development, shaping or production of a model. The result of modeling is *model provision*, which is followed by model monitoring. In relation to the field of DDM, two of these areas are particularly relevant: computer science and algorithmics.

2.37 Model monitoring

Model monitoring defines the section of machine learning after model deployment. Within model monitoring, models are monitored for errors, crashes and inconsistencies, and latencies. Model monitoring must ensure that the results reach an ever-higher level in terms of *objectivity, reliability,* and *validity, in order* to contribute in the best possible way to yield-optimized and risk-minimized business management.

The importance of model monitoring arises from the phenomenon of *model drift*, also known as model decay, which refers to the deterioration of a model's out- and predictive power.

2.38 Sample units

Sample units are units in data sets that are used for the development, evaluation, optimization and validation of models in the context of data-driven management. A distinction is made between sample units within the sample (see In-Sample) and outside the sample (see Out-Of-Sample).

2.39 Neural networks

Neural networks represent the basis of modern automatic image recognition. There are three main factors that make them relevant for data-driven management:

- Optimized storage and availability of data
- Increased and rapidly evolving computing power
- New algorithms

Neural networks use or work in layers, where the result of one layer represents the input for the next layer. A distinction is made between the following types of layers:

- Input layers
- Intermediate layers or hidden layers
- Output layers
- Loss layers

2.40 Out-of-Sample

In contrast to the term in-sample, sample or training units in samples with known attributes but unknown causal properties are referred to as out-of-sample. These out-of-sample units are not necessarily related to the training sample units in terms of content logic.

2.41 Parameter

Parameters are ways of changing the settings of an algorithm, as in the case of a kitchen stove where the temperature of a single hotplate is set. This fact leads to the fact that one and the same algorithm can deliver different results depending on how its parameters are set. Since in the field of data-driven management models are very often very powerful and complex, the complexity can be kept under control by means of the regularization process.

2.42 Predictive analysis

Predictive analytics (PA) is a subfield and also one of the pillars of *business analytics*. PA falls into the area of *data mining* . PA is used to calculate probabilities for the future and to identify corresponding trends. By using so-called *predictors* (see the corresponding section 2.44), these predictions about the future can be made very precisely. By using several, different predictors, a prediction model is created to calculate probable events.

In recent years, PA has also become established in the context of *predictive profit marketing* (Seebacher 2020). PA involves the application of statistical analysis techniques, analytical queries, and automated machine learning algorithms to data sets.

The PA generally distinguishes between three models, which are discussed in more detail in the various sections of the PI Ecosystem:

1. Prediction models or predictive models (see Predictive models)
2. Descriptive models (see Descriptive models)
3. Decision models

2.43 Predictive models or modeling

Predictive models use methods from mathematics and computer science. It is about the prediction of future events or outcomes. These models are developed in an iterative process with a training data set and training patterns, tested and evaluated with respect to the accuracy of the generated predictions. In recent years, technologies from the field of artificial intelligence and machine learning have also been increasingly used in the area of predictive models in order to identify the most optimal and valid one from several models.

2.44 Predictors

Predictors are variables in an equation that are used to forecast future events.

2.45 Prescriptive analytics

Prescriptive analytics can be defined as a subset of data analytics in which predictive models are used to suggest concrete actions. These recommended actions are, in turn, contextually aligned with the optimal outcome in each case, which was described or determined as part of the project definition initially performed. Prescriptive analytics rely on optimization and rule-based decision-making techniques. Prescriptive analytics adds a real-time element to predictive analytics results by applying actions to events. Artun and Levin (2015) define three methods of prescriptive analytics:

- Unsupervised learning (clustering models)
- Supervised learning (predictive models)
- Reinforcement learning (recommendation models)

2.46 Predictive marketing

So far, this term has not been used congruently in the literature, nor has it been definitively defined accordingly. Artun and Levin (2015) write in this regard:

> "Predictive analytics refers to a set of tools and algorithms used to enable predictive marketing. It is an umbrella term that encompasses a variety of mathematical and statistical techniques to identify patterns in data or make predictions about the future. When applied to marketing, predictive analytics can predict future customer behavior, categorize customers into clusters and into other use cases. Predictive marketing is the perfect marriage between machine learning and human intelligence. "

Molly Galetto of NG Data defines predictive marketing this way:[3]

> "Predictive marketing is a marketing technique that uses data analytics to determine which marketing strategies and promotions have the highest likelihood of success. It has its place in the marketing technology (MarTech) landscape as companies use general business data, marketing and sales activity data, and mathematical algorithms to match patterns and

---

[3] https://www.ngdata.com/what-is-predictive-marketing/. Accessed and translated: April 12, 2021

determine the most appropriate criteria for their next marketing actions. Companies adopting this strategy strive to make data-driven decisions to drive better results."

Galetto thus provides a generally applicable definition, which at the same time also provides the transfer to the broader field of corporate management and the strategy belonging to it. It focuses on data-driven decisions to achieve better results - from marketing but of course in relation to the entire company.

2.47 Procurement Intelligence

Procurement Intelligence (ProcI) is closely linked to data-driven business management. Procurement Intelligence is also based on a multidimensional data cube structured by applications, industries, and regions, which roughly divides potential suppliers into three target categories: price, delivery time, and special requirements in terms of size, processing, material, etc. ProcI is also based on a data cube structured by applications, industries, and regions.

ProcI automatically weights the relevant information and thus always delivers a selection of relevant potential suppliers - faster, more valid and always up-to-date. Procurement intelligence is defined as follows (Seebacher 2021):

> "Procurement Intelligence is the IT-based collection, processing, validation of 24/7 interactive provision of data and information on relevant suppliers in order to always be able to achieve an optimal Return-on-Procurement (RoP) situationally and according to the various criteria of price, delivery time and special requirements with regard to gestation."

2.48 Random Forrest

The term is based on the hypothesis that combining models improves predictive accuracy. Such a combination is referred to as *ensembling* or *ensemble learning*. A Random Forrest refers to a bundle of decision trees, where the bundle in this context is an aggregate, synergistic predictive model. Such a model is created by combining many different individual models either through majority voting or averaging. Two methods are used in the Random Forrest framework:

- Bootstrap aggregating generates a large number of uncorrelated decision trees by randomly eliminating some variables.
- Ensembling combines several decision trees or their predictions by mathematical methods, either majority voting or averaging.

2.49 Regression analysis

This method identifies the so-called optimal trend line[4], which touches as many data points as possible or comes as close to them as possible. This trend line is calculated using weighted combinations of *predictors*, where the regression coefficients in this context denote the corresponding weights.

2.50 Regularization

This term refers to a way to control the complexity of a model by introducing a so-called *penalty parameter*. Such a parameter "punishes" any complication of a model by artificially increasing the prediction error.

2.51 Training pattern

Training samples are used in predictive analytics to process and optimize descriptive models. In this context, a distinction is made between in-sample and out-of-sample units, which are also defined in this section.

2.52 Unsupervised learning

This form of learning is used in the field of machine learning, such as *Deep Learning*, where learning on the hierarchies or layers hidden in the system cannot be traced from the outside. Unsupervised learning therefore defines machine learning without target values known ex ante. Machines attempt to detect patterns in the data that deviate from the structureless rest of the data population (Hinton and Sejnowksi 1999). Various things can be learned in unsupervised learning, but most importantly, automatic segmentation (clustering) and compression of data for dimensionality reduction find application.

2.53 Supervised learning

In contrast to unsupervised learning, in supervised learning an ex-ante defined learning algorithm tries to find a hypothesis that predicts as accurately as possible. This method is thus guided by a task to be learned that is defined in advance and whose results are known. The results of the learning process are compared with the known, correct results, i.e., "supervised" (Müller and Guido 2017). The following methods, among others, are used in supervised learning:

---

[4] Best fit trend line or regression line

- Linear regression
- Logistic regression
- Bayes classifier
- Naive Bayes classifier
- Nearest neighbor classification
- Discriminant analysis
- Artificial neural network

2.54 Validation

This term refers to testing the precision with which a model generates predictions for new data. This approach can be used to determine the best model in the context of the DDM that provides the most accurate predictions for the test data set.

2.55 Variables

In formal language, the term in logic refers to a placeholder for different expressions. In the context of data-driven management, it is used to define a placeholder for unknowns, indeterminates, or variables in formulations, formulas, and even algorithms. There are four basic types of variables, which Seebacher (2021) describes and interprets in more detail:

- Binary
- Qualitative
- Integer or discrete
- Steady

2.56 The dynamics of the DDM conceptual world

The half-life in today's practice but also in science is characterized by an increasing dynamic. This chapter has briefly and concisely covered the currently most important terms in the context of data-driven management.

Data-driven management is a young discipline in which more and more experts from a wide variety of disciplines are coming together in order to be able to provide companies and their managers with the necessary basis for sustainable and responsible corporate management and control in the sense of fulfilling basic economic principles. At this point, no claim is made to completeness, since the only constant is change.

Further reading

Artun, Ö., & Levin, D. (2015). Predictive marketing-Easy ways every marketer can use. Hoboken: Wiley.
Blondel, V. D., Guillaume, J.-L., Lambiotte, R., & Lefebvre, E. (2008). *Fast unfolding of communities in large networks.* Journal of Statistical Mechanics: Theory and Experiment, 2008(10), P10008.
Borgelt, C., Klawonn, F., Kruse, R., & Nauck, D. (2003). Neuro-fuzzy systems-From the foundations of artificial neural networks to coupling with fuzzy systems. Cham: Springer.
Bruderer, H. (2018). *Invention of the computer, electron computer, developments in Germany, England and Switzerland.* In Milestones in computing technology (2nd, completely revised and greatly expanded edition. Vol. 2). Munich: De Gruyter.
Chamoni, P., & Gluchowski, P. (2006). *Analytical information systems: Business intelligence technologies and applications* (3rd ed.). Berlin: Springer. Christl, W. (2014, November). Commercial digital surveillance in everyday life. PDF. at: crackedlabs.org, p. 12.
Dhar, V. (2013). *Data science and prediction.* Communications of the ACM, 56(12), 64.
Dinter, B., & Winter, R. (Eds.). (2008). *Integrated information logistics (business engineering).* Heidelberg: Springer.
Escoufier, Y., et al. (1995). Preface. In Data science and its application (englisch). London: Academic Press.
Fayyad, U. M., Piatetsky-Shapiro, G., & Smyth, P. (1996). *From data mining to knowledge discovery in databases.* AI Magazine, 17(3), S. 37-54.
Felden, C., & Buder, J. (2012). *Decision support in network societies.* Information Systems, 1, pp. 17-32.
Forbes. (2013). A very short history of data science. New Jersey: Gil Press.
Gareth, J., Witten, D., Hastie, T., & Tibshirani, R. (2017). *An introduction to statistical learning with applications in R.* New York: Springer.
Güpner, A. (2015). I'm a star – Let me in here! The career book for the perfect career start. Munich: USP International.
Hinton, G., & Sejnowski, T. J. (Hrsg.). (1999). *Unsupervised learning: Foundations of neural computation.* Cambridge: MIT Press.
IIBA® International Institute of Business Analysis. (2017). BABOK® v3 guide to *business analysis BABOK® Guide 3.0* (3rd, expanded edition). Giessen: Verlag Dr. Götz Schmidt.
Müller, A. C., & Guido, S. (2017). Introduction to machine learning with Python: practical knowledge data science. Heidelberg: O'Reilly.
Ng, A., & Soo, K. (2018). Data science-what is it! Machine learning algorithms. Learning explained in an understandable way. Berlin: Springer.
Reichert, R. (2014). Big Data: Analyses on the digital transformation of knowledge, power and economy. Bielefeld: Transcript Verlag.
Rifkin, J. (2019). The global Green New Deal: Why fossil-fueled civilization will collapse around 2028-and a bold economic plan can save life on Earth. Frankfurt: Campus Verlag.
Seebacher, U. (2020). B2B marketing: A guidebook for the classroom to the boardroom. Cham: Springer.
Seebacher, U. (2020b). Template-based management – A guide for efficient and effective professional practice. Graz: AQPS Inc.
Seebacher, U. (2021). Predictive Intelligence for Managers – The easy way to data-driven business management – with self-assessment, procedure model and case studies. Heidelber: Springer.
Smola, A. (2008). *Introduction to machine learning.* Cambridge: Cambridge University Press.
Strohmeier, L. (2020). *Central business intelligence.* In U. Seebacher (Hrsg.), B2B marketing –A guidebook for the classroom to the boardroom. Cham: Springer.
Wiggins, R. (1992). *Docking a truck: A genetic fuzzy approach.* AI Expert, 7(5), 28-35.

The DDM Self-Assessment   3

This chapter describes and presents the test procedure that can be used to determine in and or predictive intelligence as a DDM target dimension. This self-assessment is based on the previously described DDM maturity model and maps all required dimensions.

If not only one person from an organization completes the assessment for a given organization, but the generated result can also be validated on the basis of a divergence analysis. If there is little divergence between the values generated in each case, one can assume high validity, whereas with increasing divergence the validity of the results decreases and should be questioned.

3.1   The dimensions of the DDM assessment

The assessment is divided into eight content elements, which are underpinned by different sets of questions:

1. Potential Index
2. Value Chain Index
3. Cost Efficiency Index
4. Structure index
5. Strategy index
6. Distribution Index
7. Infrastructure Index
8. Competence Index

Based on these eight areas, a corresponding spider chart can be generated from the responses, showing very clearly at a glance how a US-based benchmark organization is scoring in terms of data-driven management (Fig. 3.1).

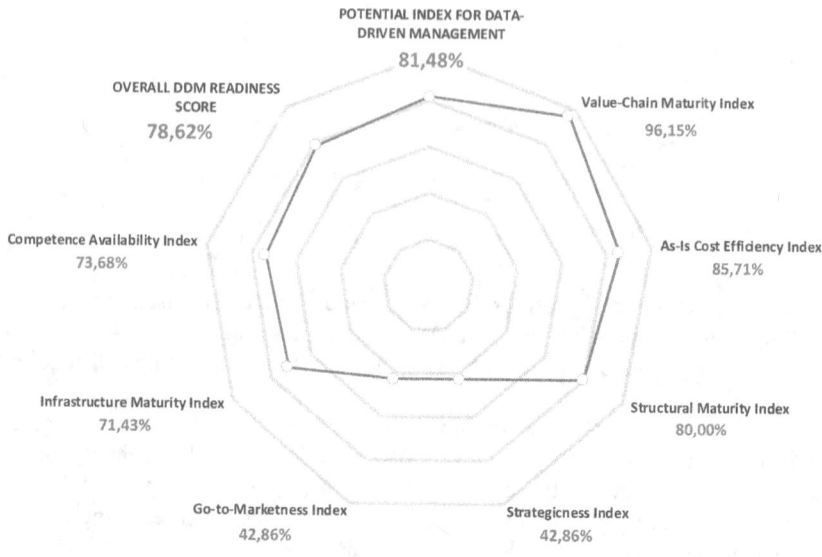

Fig. 3.1. Benchmark evaluation of a DDM showcase company (source: Seebacher 2021).

Figure 3.1. shows the status of an organization that is already very highly developed in terms of DDM. The spider graph shows, on the one hand, how great the potential for DDM of this organization is (91.3%) and, on the other hand, how far the various index areas could be developed in the course of the three-year project without any specifically required budgets. In the following sections, this example evaluation will be referenced again and again in order to better illustrate and clarify the values and their statement.

3.1.1 The potential index

Is it worthwhile for an organization to invest in data-driven management or predictive intelligence? The Potential Index uses six structural questions to determine how great the potential for data-driven corporate management of an organization is by asking in how many industries, regions or countries the unit in question is active. In addition, the question is about the number of products offered for which applications. The more heterogeneous an organization's offering is on the one hand, and the multitude of different markets on the other, the more important it is to act very precisely on the basis of predictive intelligence in a sustainable manner. The more areas an organization is active in, the more extensive and complex the respective contingency situations become, which in turn must be mapped and analyzed using large volumes of data, i.e., *Big Data*.

Thus, the higher the potential index, the greater the potential of an organization in relation to DDM and vice versa. In any case, a company that offers only one product in one country will derive much less long-term benefit from DDM compared to a medium-sized company with a highly disaggregated product portfolio and a global presence, as is the basis for the evaluation in Fig. 3.1. Answer the following questions to determine the PI-PI for your respective organizational unit by marking the respective answer.

Tab. 3.1 Questions on the Potential Index

No.	Question	Answer options						Pkt.
		0	1	2	3	4	5	
1	In how many industries does the organization operate?	I do not know	1	2	<5	5+		
2	On how many continents does the organization operate?	I do not know	1	2	3	4+		
3	In how many countries does the organization operate?	I do not know	1	<10	<25	25+		
4	How many products/solutions does the organization offer?	I do not know	<5	<25	<50	50+		
5	How many production sites does the organization have?	I do not know	None	<5	<15	15+		
6	What is the percentage of fraudulent business transactions?	<0,1%	0,1 – 0,3%	0,3 – 0,5%	0,5 – 1%	1 – 3%	3 – 5%	
7	What is the current set-up in terms of marketing, product mgmt/marketing, business development and sales?	I do not know	In one unit	2 or more in one unit	All single			
8	What is the organization's marketing strategy?	B2C	B2B	B2G [5]				

3.1.2 The value chain index

The value chain as a methodical and sophisticated tool allows the activities of a relevant organizational unit to be analyzed comprehensively and consistently. The value chain is thus the link between the operational and the conceptual-structural level.

Within the framework of the DDM, thinking in terms of value chains plays a very decisive role. Experience has shown that the majority of companies only cover parts of industrial value chains in terms of their product portfolio. As a result, figures, data and facts about markets and industries present a false picture.

---

[5] Business-to-Government

Tab. 3.2 Questions on the value chain index

No.	Question	Answer options						Pkt.
		0	1	2	3	4	5	
9	Are you already using VC[6] to analyze, customize, develop, plan and structure industry-specific offerings?	I do not know	no	partly	Yes			
10	Does the organization have cleanly researched, consistent and valid documented VCs for all industries and segments covered?	I do not know	no	partly	Yes			
11	How are these VCs developed?	I do not know	External through consultants	Together with consultant	internal			
12	How are these VC documentations updated?	I do not know	External through consultants	Together with consultant	internal			
13	How often is this VC documentation updated?	I do not know	never	Every two years	annual	More often or continuously		
14	Who is responsible for the VC work?	I do not know	other	Distribution	Prod. Mgt./Mkt.	Marketing		
15	Who is involved in the VC work?	I do not know	Only the responsible team	2 or more teams	All relevant internal stakeholders	Situational and flexible integration depending on the VAC		
16	What data is used for VC work?	I do not know	External data only	Internal data only	Internal and external data			

For example, if the global mining market had a volume XM - the *absolute market* - and consisted of a three-part value chain of mining (XA), transport (XT), processing (XV) - thus $XM=f_{(A+T+V)}$, then the *relevant market* for a supplier of submersible pumps, which are only used in the first part of the industrial value chain in mining, would no longer be XM, but $XA=f_{(M-T-V)}$. It follows that the relevant market is in any case smaller and different from the absolute market. In this context, the relevant market in turn depends on the respective product portfolio of the company under investigation. Therefore, if the structure of the relevant industrial value chain is not taken into account, the figures used are wrong and too high, which can have

---

[6] VC is used as an abbreviation for value chain here for ease of reading.

fatal consequences for investment decisions as well as for the evaluation of the company's own market share.

Against this background, it is fundamental to map the industries served by an organization in the form of value chains. This involves determining the annual investments in machinery and equipment (*CAPEX*) but also in ongoing service and maintenance costs (*OPEX*) per defined section of the value chain. The second set of questions in the PI-SA therefore measures the maturity of an organization in dealing with the relevant industrial value chains.

3.1.3 The cost efficiency index

The development of an own DDM infrastructure offers enormous cost advantages, as this is also made clear by the maturity model. This is because, in addition to many other effects and benefits, an internal, organization owned DDM can replace external information and newsletter services very quickly and easily at the lowest possible cost. These significant savings can be used directly for the development of own competencies or employees, but also for the purchase of further industry-specific data.

The value of the example organization in terms of KE-I with 85.71% shows that more than three quarters of the costs have already been converted from external and short-term to internal and sustainable. For example, all external newsletter service provider subscriptions were cancelled at the earliest possible date and high six-figure euro amounts were immediately saved. These were used to purchase additional data from pre-selected and pre-qualified sources to expand the internal data pool for the development of time series and corresponding analyses. Answer the questions in table 3.3.

3.1.4 The structure index

As a structural starting point for DDM, this can be the Market and Business Intelligence (MI/BI) team or a central department in the *corporate development* environment. In rare cases, *Central Intelligence* (Strohmeier, 2020) units already exist. The current study by Freeform Dynamics Ltd. (2020) confirms this assessment, as around half of the companies currently use any form of data at all to support corporate management. Answer the questions on the structures in table 3.4.

3.1.5 The strategy index

Building on the structure index, the strategy index (tab. 3.5) examines the extent to which the topic of corporate strategy is defined and organized. DDM focuses not only on short- and medium-term aspects of corporate management, but also and especially on strategic issues on the basis of increasingly precise and extrapolable multidimensional data. However, in order to develop the appropriate competence

Tab. 3.3 Questions on the cost efficiency index

No.	Question	Answer options						
		0	1	2	3	4	5	Pkt.
17	What percentage of the marketing budget is currently spent on Market/Bus. Intelligence (MI/BI)?	I do not know	<2%	2 – 5%	5 – 10%	+10%		
18	How often are updates sent to the organization in the form of an MI/BI newsletter?	I do not know	Not at all	Irregular	Regular (e.g. ¼-yearly, 2-monthly, monthly)	Monthly		
19	How many external analyses, reports, studies, etc. are purchased per year on average?	I do not know	20 and more	10 - 20	5 - 10	<5		
20	What is the average cost of these external reports per piece?	I do not know	25.000 Euro or more	10.000 - 25.000 Euro	5.000 - 25.000 Euro	Less than 5,000 euros		
21	How many external service providers for data, information, newsletters/updates, etc. are currently contracted?	I do not know	5 or more	2 to 5	Less than 2	0		
22	What is the approximate cost of these service providers per year in euros?	I do not know	100,000 or more	50.000 – 100.000	25.000 – 50.000	Less than 25,000		
23	Which department provides the budget for this?	I do not know	Several departments	Distribution	MI/BI only	Marketing only		

Tab. 3.4 Questions on the structure index

No.	Question	Answer options						
		0	1	2	3	4	5	Pkt.
24	Is the MI/BI function located in marketing?	I do not know	No	Yes				
25	If NO, where is MI/BI currently located?	I do not know	Distribution	Other department				
26	If YES, how often does sales request MI/BI support?	I do not know	Monthly	Weekly	Several times a week			
27	If YES, is MI/BI information available 24/7 online, interactively for sales?	I do not know	No	Partial	Yes			

with regard to strategic aspects of data-driven corporate management, it is essential to start at the operational level. In this context, the preparation and establishment of predictive intelligence must therefore also take into account how the broad and important topic of strategy is currently set up in organizations. The strategy index is mapped and defined from an organizational perspective based on the following questions.

Tab. 3.5 Strategy index questions

No.	Question	Answer options						Pkt.
		0	1	2	3	4	5	
28	Is the topic of strategy located in marketing?	I do not know	No	Yes				
29	If NO, where is the issue currently located?	I do not know	Distribution	Other department				
30	If YES, how often does sales request strategy support?	I do not know	Monthly	Weekly	Several times a week			

3.1.6 The distribution index

Crucial in the context of DDM is the area of future business development. Therefore, the questions in the topic area of the Distribution Index focus on the area of *Business Development,* as this function must define and identify where, when and how services and products of an organization are to be distributed in relevant markets.

It is not just a question of distribution in terms of content, but rather distribution in terms of marketing, in order to generate as many *inbound leads* as possible (Wenger, 2020). Inbound leads are incoming inquiries for products and concrete offers generated by marketing. Such inquiries have an extremely positive effect on the respective *return on sales* (RoS), because in this way cost- and time-intensive cold calling can be bypassed. Modern industrial goods marketing can now cover large parts of the sales process in an automated manner in order to only involve sales when inquiries have been concretized and validated to such an extent that the timeframe, decision maker and budget for the purchase decision are clearly defined. To do this, answer the questions in Table 3.6.

Tab. 3.6 Questions on the distribution index

No.	Question	Answer options						Pkt.
		0	1	2	3	4	5	
31	Is the topic of business development located in marketing?	I do not know	No	Yes				
32	If NO, where is the issue currently located?	I do not know	Distribution	Other department				
33	If YES, how often does sales request business development support?	I do not know	Monthly	Weekly	Several times a week			

3.1.7 The infrastructure index

In order to start establishing DDM in an organization, no special applications or tools are actually required initially. The infrastructure index (Tab. 3.7) therefore determines which useful applications can be drawn upon in the context of establishing DDM. The higher this value, the better and more comprehensive the PI-relevant infrastructure already present in the organization under investigation.

Tab. 3.7 Questions on the infrastructure index

No.	Question	Answer options						Pkt.
		0	1	2	3	4	5	
34	Does the organization have a 24/7 intranet available worldwide?	I do not know	No	Yes				
35	Does the organization have an organization-wide CRM system?	I do not know	No	Yes				
36	Does the organization have an organization-wide ERP system?	I do not know	No	Yes				
37	Does the organization have an organization-wide business intelligence system?[7]	I do not know	No	Yes				
38	Does the organization have an organization-wide marketing automation system?[8]	I do not know	No	Yes				
39	Does the organization have an organization-wide lead scanning system?	I do not know	No	Yes				
40	Does the organization have a configure-price-quote system available organization-wide?[9]	I do not know	No	Yes				

3.1.8 The competence index

The last index in the DDM assessment helps to determine the current status with regard to operational competencies (Tab. 3.8). The earlier one is aware of the necessary knowledge areas, the earlier one can begin to develop these topics internally.

3.2 The evaluation of the DDM assessment

We have now answered all segments of the Predictive Intelligence Self-Assessment in terms of content. In the following, we will now evaluate the previously given answers. To do this, enter the points given in the second row for each answer in the

---

[7] Common business intelligence solutions include Click, PowerBI, SAP Analytics Cloud or Tableau.
[8] Common marketing automation solutions include Hubspot or Adobe's Marketo.
[9] https://de.wikipedia.org/wiki/Configure_Price_Quote. Accessed: April 14, 2021

Tab. 3.8 Questions on the competence index

No.	Question	Answer options						Pkt.
		0	1	2	3	4	5	
41	Does the organization have a data science manager (DSM)?	I do not know	No	Partial	Yes			
42	Does the organization have a content asset manager (CAM)?	I do not know	No	Partial	Yes			
43	Does the organization have a Marketing Campaign Manager (MCM)?	I do not know	No	Partial	Yes			
44	Does the organization have a marketing operations manager (MOM)?	I do not know	No	Partial	Yes			
45	Does the organization have a marketing performance manager (MPM)?	I do not know	No	Partial	Yes			
46	Does the organization have a marketing technology manager (MTM)?	I do not know	No	Partial	Yes			
47	At what level is the senior vice president or director of marketing or CMO positioned in relation to the board?	I do not know	3 or more levels below	2 levels below	1 level below	At board level		
48	At what level is the Head of Marketing positioned in relation to the Executive Board?	I do not know	3 or more levels below	2 levels below	1 level below	At board level		

Tab. 3.9 Sample evaluation for the distribution index

No.	Question	Answer options						Pkt.
		0	1	2	3	4	5	
31	Is the topic of business development located in marketing?	I do not know	No	Yes				1
32	If NO, where is the issue currently located?	I do not know	Distribution	Other department				2
33	If YES, how often does sales request business development support?	I do not know	Monthly	Weekly	Several times a week			

various tables so that the entire rightmost column is filled with scores. An example of a pre-filled table is shown here (Tab. 3.9).

Based on the answers entered, the value "1" was taken for the right-hand column named "Pkt." in the second row for question 31. For question 32, the value "2" was used accordingly. This results in the table number for the D-I in this case being 3 and, on this basis, in relation to the total, possible maximum value of 5, a percentage value of 60%. The maximum value of "5" results from the answer "Yes" to question 31, which is assigned the value "2", and the answer "Several times a week" to question 33 - question 32 can only be answered in the case of a "No" to question 31 - which is assigned the value "3".

Using the same procedure, all tables (3.1 to 3.8) are now to be completed in the next step and the respective table totals are to be transferred to table 3.10.

To determine the *Overall Readiness Score,* the percentage values of tables 3.2 to 3.8 must be added together and then divided by the number 7. This determined value is then related to the value in Table 3.1. The following calculation (Tab. 3.11) must be performed.

In the last step of Table 3.11, the RS is determined for the organization under investigation, which is then entered in the corresponding field in the spider graph, as are the other index values, to complete the self-assessment for DDM (Fig. 3.2). Thus, the DDM maturity level for the relevant organizational unit is now defined and the status quo shows where one can or must start from.

Tab. 3.10 Evaluation table index segments

Table	Table name	Achieved table points (T_E)	Maximum achievable table points (T_M)	Determination of index value (T_E/T_M)*100
3.1	PI	_____	30	_____/30 _____/100 %
3.2	WK-I	_____	27	_____/27 _____/100 %
3.3	KE-I	_____	28	_____/28 _____/100 %
3.4	SR-I	_____	8	_____/8 _____/100 %
3.5	SA-I	_____	5	_____/5 _____/100 %
3.6	D-I	_____	5	_____/5 _____/100 %
3.7	I2	_____	14	_____/14 _____/100 %
3.8	AI	_____	26	_____/26 _____/100 %

Tab. 3.11 Evaluation table Overall Readiness Score (RS)

Table	Table name	Determination of index value $(TE/TM)*100$	Intermediate values	
3.1	PI	____/30 ____/100 %		
3.2	WK-I	____/27 ____/100 %		
3.3	KE-I	____/28 ____/100 %		
3.4	SR-I	____/8 ____/100 %	____/113 ____/100%	Percentage value Tab. 3.2 - 3.8 divided by Percentage PI
3.5	SA-I	____/5 ____/100 %		
3.6	D-I	____/5 ____/100 %		_____
3.7	I2	____/14 ____/100 %		
3.8	AI	____/26 ____/100 %		

Based on the projects realized, a semi-annual PI Self Assessment can be helpful for reflecting on one's own development. As already discussed, the involvement of internal customers is certainly also an important aspect in order to obtain a valid picture of the situation with regard to the maturity level for predictive intelligence.

3.3 Knowing where you stand

This section described the compass that makes it possible to take the right path right from the start. Time and again, the topic of data-driven business management and

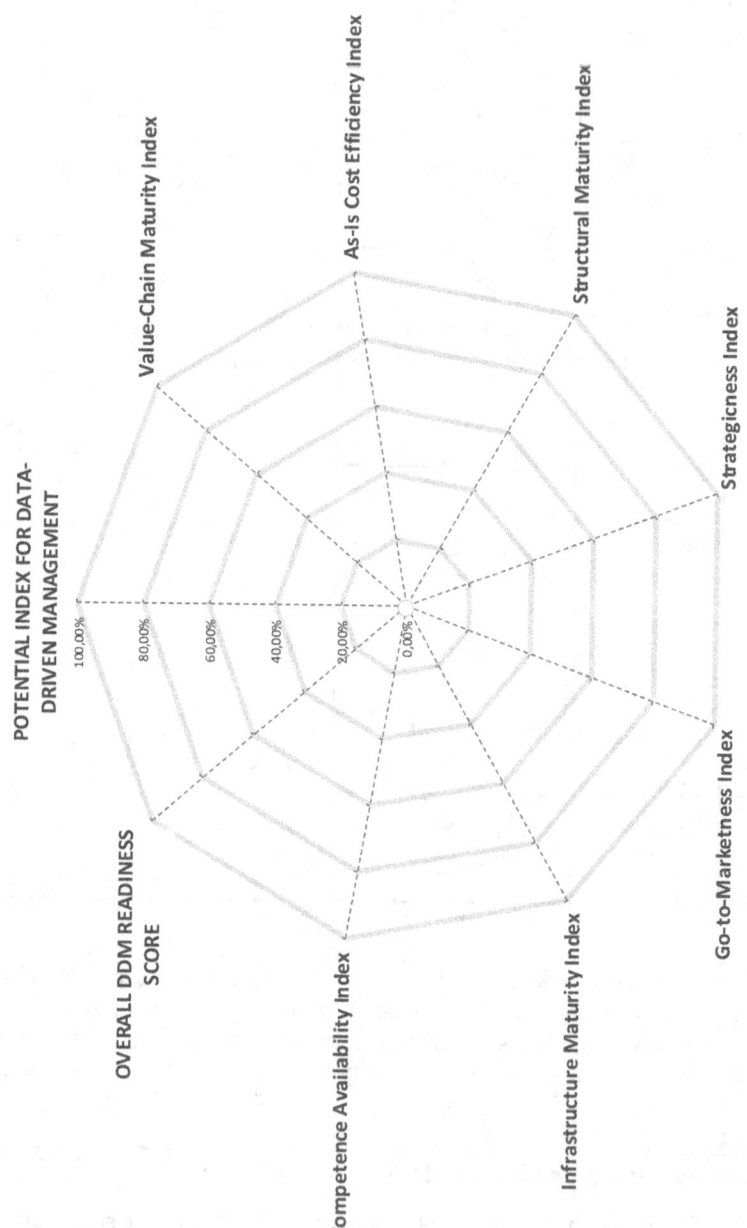

Fig. 3.2 Spider grid for the DDM self-assessment (source: own representation).

even more so the new field of predictive intelligence is unnecessarily mystified. As always in life, it requires an eye for the big picture, but also the appropriate basic skills.

The DDM Self-Assessment is intended to be a simple but all the more helpful tool for deepening the necessary sensitivity with regard to relevant organizational, but also instrumental and competence-theoretical factors.

Further reading

Cummings, T. (2013). *Everything you need to know about dynamic pricing*. The Christian Science Monitor.
Freeform Dynamics Ltd. (2020). *The road to becoming a data-driven business*. Research report.
Harting, D. (1994). *Value creation on new paths*. Beschaffung aktuell. 7/1994.
Kotler, P., et al. (2007). *Marketing management: Strategies for value creation* (12th ed. Edition). Munich: Pearson Studium.
Seebacher, U. (2020a). *B2B marketing: A guidebook for the classroom to the boardroom*. Cham: Springer.
Seebacher, U. (2020b). *B2B marketing essential: How to turn your marketing from a cost into a sales engine* (2nd ed.). Graz: AQPS.
Seebacher, U. (2020c). *Template-based management-A guide for an efficient and impactful professional practice*. Cham: Springer.
Strohmeier, L. (2020). *Central business intelligence*. In U. Seebacher (Hrsg.), B2B marketing-A guidebook for the classroom to the boardroom. Cham: Springer.
Wenger, St. (2020). *Erfolgreiches lead management*. In U. Seebacher (Hrsg.), B2B marketing-A guidebook for the classroom to the boardroom. Cham: Springer.

Summary and outlook

In the context of this book, an attempt was made to bring a seemingly complex topic of modern management practice to the point in a concise and pointed manner. The goal was to demystify this topic, which is so important for corporate survival. Albert Einstein said:

> "If you can't **explain** it **easily**, you didn't understand it well enough!"

Following this premise, we have focused on the essentials to realize this guide for data-driven management. In the meantime, many practitioners have used this guide to very successfully master the first steps of the process model to DDM in the direction of data-driven management to overcome the currently dominant data blindness in companies. At this point, we can only encourage them to take up this extremely fascinating challenge together with their teams. After all, anyone who questions the necessity of DDM these days is obviously not keeping up with the times and is also moving with the times.

The extended version of this essential on DDM can be found in our book "Predictive Intelligence for Data-driven Managers – Process Model, Assessment-Tool, IT-Blueprint, Competence Model and Case Studies (Springer 2021). At this point, it should be noted that there is excellent further literature on this topic, which also provides valuable information and tips from applied research and practical work without the necessary prior knowledge. We have listed these in the relevant chapters of this book. In addition, renowned associations, institutions and media houses now offer specific programs for developing but also deepening DDM-specific knowledge. Via the following links, relevant programs and courses can be found in the context of DDM:

- **Federal Association of Industrial Communication:** https://bvik.org/b2b-kompetenz-werkstatt/datengetriebenes-management-hands-on-erlernen/#detail
- **Iversity Springer:** https://iversity.org/de/courses/data-management-excellence-journey

With this in mind, we wish you every success on the journey towards data-driven management. Success, as always, is the result of many small steps. Be brave, stay grateful and look after your physical, but also mental health.

What you can take away from this *essential*

- An up-to-date overview of the dynamic field of data-driven management.
- The maturity model that should be your guide and reference for the challenges and issues of your everyday life.
- An easy-to-perform, effective DDM readiness assessment that helps you see where you currently stand with your organization and where you need to start.
- The realization that as a manager and leader you must actively shape your own future and the sustainable positioning of your organization
- The need to understand data as the new gold and to establish this fact accordingly in management.
- The realization that any business decision can and must only be made more and exclusively on objective, reliable and valid data.
- An e-mail address where you can reach me at any time.

Additional literature

Artun, Ö., Levin D. (2015): Predictive Marketing - Easy Ways Every Marketer Can Use., Wiley, New Jersey.
Bacon, A. (2020): Account-based Marketing. in: Seebacher, U. (Hrsg.): Praxishandbuch B2B Marketing. Springer, Heidelberg.
Barron, J. M., Berger, M. C., Black, D. A. (1997): Introduction to On-the-Job Training. Upjohn Institute for Employment Research. S. 1-3.
Becker, G. S. (1993): Human Capital - A Theoretical and Empirical Analysis with Special Reference to Education. 3. Auflage. University of Chicago Press. Chicago.
Blondel, V. D., Guillaume, J.-L., Lambiotte, R., Lefebvre, E. (2008): Fast unfolding of communities in large networks. Journal of Statistical Mechanics: Theory and Experiment. 2008 (10): P10008
Borgelt, Ch., Klawonn, F., Kruse, R., Nauck D.: Neuro-Fuzzy-Systeme - Von den Grundlagen künstlicher Neuronaler Netze zur Kopplung mit Fuzzy-Systemen. Springer, Wiesbaden.
Branbandt, N. (2016): Solving the leadership problem - Developing an effective and sustainable leadership model based on the experiences of management and leadership thought leaders. Academia Education, London.
Bruderer, H. (2018): Invention of the computer, electron computer, developments in Germany, England and Switzerland. In: Milestones in computing technology. 2nd, completely revised and greatly expanded edition. Vol. 2. De Gruyter, Berlin.
Brynjolfsson, E., Collis, A.: "The value of the digital economy", Harvard Business Manager, April 2020, pp. 50 - 58.
Busol, M. (2019): War for Talents: Success factors in the battle for the best. Springer Gabler. Heidelberg.
Bühner, R. (2005): Personalmanagement. 3rd ed. Oldenbourg Verlag. Munich.
Chamoni, P., Gluchowski, P. (2006): Analytical Information Systems: Business intelligence technologies and applications. 3rd ed. Springer, Berlin.
Christl, W. (2014): Commercial digital surveillance in everyday life. PDF, at: crackedlabs.org, November 2014, p. 12.
Cummings, T. (2013): Everything you need to know about dynamic pricing. The Christian Science Monitor.
Dhar, V. (2013): Data science and prediction. Communications of the ACM 56 (12): 64.
Edmondson, A. C.: "The Fearless Organization - Creating Psycho-logical Safety in the Workplace for Learning, Innovation and Growth". Wiley, 2018
Ermer, B (2020): Social Selling im B2B Marketing, in: Seebacher, U.: Praxishandbuch B2B Marketing. Springer, Heidelberg.
Escoufier et al. (1995): Preface. In: Data Science and its Application (englisch). Academic Press, Tokyo.
Ester, M., Sander, J. (2000): Knowledge Discovery in Databases. Techniques and applications. Springer, Berlin.
Fayyad, U. M., Piatetsky-Shapiro G., Smyth, P. (1996): From Data Mining to Knowledge Discovery in Databases. In: AI Magazine. Band 17, Nr. 3, S. 37-54.

Felden, C., Buder, J. (2012): Decision Support in Network Societies. In: Business Informatics 1, pp. 17-32.
Forbes (2013): A Very Short History of Data Science. Gil Press.
Freeform Dynamics Ltd. (2020): The Road to Becoming A Data-driven Business - Research Report. London.
Frei, F., Morriss, A.: Unleashed. The unapologetic leader's guide to empowering everyone around you. Harvard Business Review. June 2020
Frey, A., Trenz, M., and Veit, D. (2019): A Service-Dominant Logic Perspective on the Roles of Technology in Service Innovation: Uncovering Four Archetypes in the Sharing Economy, Journal of Business Economics (89:8-9), pp. 1149-1189. (https://doi.org/10.1007/s11573-019-00948-z)
Gareth, J., Witten, D., Hastie, T., Tibshirani, R. (2017): An Introduction to Statistical Learning with Applications in R., Springer New York.
Güpner, A. (2015): Ich bin ein Star - Let me in here! The career book for the perfect career start. USP International, Munich
Halb, F.; Seebacher, U. (2020): Customer Experience und Touchpoint Management, in: Seebacher, U. (Ed.): Praxishandbuch B2B Marketing. Springer, Heidelberg.
Han, J., Kamber, M. (2001): Data mining: concepts and techniques. 1. Auflage. Morgan Kaufmann, 2001.
Harting, D. (1994): Value creation on new paths. In: Beschaffung aktuell. 7/1994.
Hildebrand, K., Gebauer, M., et al. (2018). Data and information quality: towards information excellence. Springer Vieweg. Heidelberg.
Hinton, G., Sejnowski, T. J. (Hrsg.) (1999): Unsupervised Learning: Foundations of Neural Computation. MIT Press, 1999
IIBA® International Institute of Business Analysis (2017): BABOK® v3 - Leitfaden zur Business-Analyse BABOK® Guide 3.0, 3rd, expanded edition, Verlag Dr. Götz Schmidt, Wettenberg.
Iansiti, M., Lakhani, K. R.: Technology: The Truth About Blockchain. In: HBR.org, Januar/Februar 2017.
Kotler, P., et al. (2007): Marketing management: strategies for value creation. 12th edition, Pearson Studies, New York.
Kotler, P., Pfoertsch, W., Sponholz, U. (2021): H2H Marketing - The Genesis of Human-to-Human Marketing. Springer, Heidelberg.
Langley, P. (2011): The changing science of machine learning. In: Machine Learning. Band 82, Nr. 3, 18. Februar 2011, S. 275-279.
Müller, A. C., Guido, S. (2017): Introduction to Machine Learning with Python: Praxiswissen Data Science. O'Reilly, Heidelberg.
Müller, E. (2019): The Netflix industry. Manage Magazine, July 2019, pp. 95-97.
Nefiodov, L. (2014): The sixth Kondratieff: The new long wave of the world economy. The long waves of economic activity and their basic innovation. Rhein-Sieg-Vlg Nefiodow; 7th edition.
Negovan, M. (2020): 365 Tage Marketing Turnaround, in: Seebacher, U. (Ed.): Praxishandbuch B2B Marketing - Neueste Konzepte, Strategien und Technologien sowie praxiserprobte Vorgehensmodelle - mit 11 Fallstudien. Springer Verlag, Heidelberg.
Ng, A., Soo, K. (2018): Data Science - what is it anyway! Machine learning algorithms explained in an understandable way. Springer, Heidelberg.
Peter, L. J., Hull, R. (1972): Das Peter-Prinzip oder die Hierarchie der Unfähigen, Reinbek bei Hamburg.
Porter, M. E. (1986): Competitive Advantage. Achieving and maintaining top performance. Translated from the English by Angelika Jaeger. Campus Verlag, Frankfurt am Main.
Reichert, R. (2014): Big Data: Analysen zum digitalen Wandel von Wissen, Macht und Ökonomie. transcript Verlag, Bielefeld, p. 9.
Rifkin, J. (2019): The global Green New Deal: Why fossil-fueled civilization will collapse around 2028 - and a bold economic plan can save life on Earth. Campus Verlag, Frankfurt am Main.
Scheer, P., Kasper, H. (2011): Leadership und soziale Kompetenz. Linde Verlag, Vienna.

Seebacher, U. (2020): Praxishandbuch B2B Marketing - Neueste Konzepte, Strategien und Technologien sowie praxiserprobte Vorgehensmodelle - mit 11 Fallstudien. Springer Verlag, Heidelberg.
Seebacher, U. (2020): Template-based Management - A Guide to Efficient and Effective Professional Practice. AQPS Inc, Graz.
Seebacher, U. (1996): Evaluating the Efficiency of Quality Certification Using the Example of the Financial Services Sector. Dissertation at the Vienna University of Economics and Business Administration at the Institute for Technology and Production Management, Vienna.
Seebacher, U., Güpner, A. (2010): Strategic Workforce Management. USP Publishing, Munich.
Seebacher, U., Güpner, A. (2011): Marketing Resource Management. USP Publishing, Munich.
Seebacher, U., Güpner, A. (2014): Innovation durch strategisches Personalmanagement: Das "Made in Germany" sichern durch Workforce und Diversity Management. USP International, Munich - New York.
Shapiro, C., Varian, H. R. (1998): Information Rule: A Strategic Guide to the Network Economy. Harvard Business School Press, Harvard.
Smola, A. (2008): Introduction to Machine Learning. Cambridge University Press, Cambridge.
Strohmeier, L. (2020): Central Business Intelligence, in: Seebacher, U. (Ed.): Praxishandbuch B2B Marketing. Springer, Heidelberg.
Steinmetz, R.; Wehrle K. (2006): Peer-to-peer networking & computing. Current buzzword. In: Informatik Spektrum. Springer, Heidelberg 27.2004,1, 51-54.
Sturm, A., Opferbeck, I., Gurt, J. (2011): Organisational psychology, VS Verlag für Sozialwissenschaften. Wiesbaden
Vollenweider, M. (2017): mind + machine - A Decision Model for Optimizing and Implementing Analytics. Wiley India, New Delhi.
Weinländer, M. (2020): Corporate Influencing und Thought Leadership, in: Seebacher, U. (Ed.): Praxishandbuch B2B Marketing. Springer, Heidelberg
Wenger, St. (2020): Erfolgreiches Lead Management, in: Seebacher, U. (Ed.): Praxishandbuch B2B Marketing. Springer, Heidelberg
Wessel, K. F. (1998): Humanontogenetik - Neue Überlegungen zu alten Fragen. USP Publishing Kleine Verlag, Bielefeld-Munich.
Wierse, A.; Riedel, T. (2017): Smart Data Analytics (English). De Gruyter Oldenbourg, 2017
Wiggins, R. (1992): Docking a truck: A genetic fuzzy approach". AI Expert. 7 (5): 28–35.

www.ingramcontent.com/pod-product-compliance
Lightning Source LLC
Chambersburg PA
CBHW070314220526
45465CB00004B/1861